GW00771962

DARLING, I'M HOME!

A play by

JACK POPPLEWELL

SAMUEL

FRENCH

LONDON

NEW YORK TORONTO SYDNEY HOLLYWOOD

SAMUEL FRENCH LTD, 26 SOUTHAMPTON STREET, STRAND, LONDON WC2E 7JE, or their authorized agents, issue licences to amateurs to give performances of this play on payment of a fee. **The fee must be paid and the licence obtained before a performance is given.**

Licences are issued subject to the understanding that it shall be made clear in all advertising matter that the audience will witness an amateur performance; and that the names of the authors of the plays shall be included on all announcements and on all programmes.

The royalty fee indicated below is subject to contract and subject to variation at the sole discretion of Samuel French Ltd.

The publication of this play must not be taken to imply that it is necessarily available for performance by amateurs or professionals, either in the British Isles or overseas. Amateurs intending production must, in their own interests, make application to Samuel French Ltd or their authorized agents, for consent before starting rehearsals or booking a theatre or hall.

Basic fee for each and every performance by amateurs in the British Isles — Code K

In theatres or halls seating 600 or more the fee will be subject to negotiation

In territories overseas the fee quoted above may not apply. Application must be made to our local authorized agents, or if there is no such agent, to Samuel French Ltd, London.

Applications to perform the play by professionals should be made to ERIC GLASS LTD, 28 Berkley Square London W1.

ISBN 0 573 01591 0

CHARACTERS:

Rupert Johns
Celia Johns, his wife
Karen Johns, their daughter
Robin Nightingale
Inga Peterson
Barry Bingley-Brown
Rodney Billingham
Janet

The action of the play takes place in the drawing-room of a house in a village which is near to a town in Southern England

ACT I

Scene 1	Late afternoon on a day in early May
Scene 2	Several days later
Scene 3	A few weeks later—7 p.m.

ACT II

Scene 1	Some days later—2 p.m.
Scene 2	A few weeks later—7 p.m.

Time—the present

Please note our NEW ADDRESS:

Samuel French Ltd
52 Fitzroy Street London W1P 6JR
Tel: 01 - 387 9373

ACT I

SCENE 1

The drawing-room of a house in a village near a town in Southern England. Late afternoon on a day in May

In the back wall is an opening to a vestibule, in which overcoats and other items can be left. Beyond can be seen the outer door. A door on one side of the drawing-room leads to the kitchen, and on the opposite side are stairs to the bedrooms

When the Curtain rises Celia Johns is discovered alone, sitting on the settee, facing forwards, scowling, with her elbows on her knees and her chin in her hands. She is fortyish, very attractive. At the moment she is untidily dressed, symbolic of her dissatisfaction with life. After a moment Janet calls off

Janet (*off*) Celia!

Janet enters through the front door

(*As she enters*) Celia! (*She sees Celia*) Why can't you answer me?
Celia Because I'm not speaking to anybody.
Janet What have I done now?
Celia Nothing. It's that idiot husband of mine.
Janet What's he done?
Celia Nothing. He never does anything. I'm bored. Why should I sit here day after day wasting my talents whilst he goes to the office with no talents to waste? I'm the one with the brains. And if I hadn't any I'd still have more than he has.
Janet I suppose he isn't Britain's Number One Businessman.
Celia (*laughing bitterly*) He inherited a soap factory which started to go steadily downhill the moment he took over. Only it isn't going steadily any longer—it's rushing headlong.

The room is very untidy and Janet starts to pick up the debris

No, Janet, leave things where they are, thank you. We all know I'm a slut.
Janet Yes, dear, but today it's just a trifle below your norm.
Celia Every day he goes to what he laughingly calls work, sits, twiddles his silly thumbs and starts looking at the clock to see if it's time for lunch yet. How anybody who works so little and eats so much gets so tired and so hungry I'll never know.

Janet Mine's the same. You'd think he was a farmer.
Celia However, we have plans. Do you know what we're going to do? Swop jobs.

Janet laughs

I'm serious. We met at the office. I was a damn good secretary, and he isn't good at anything. At least, not in the office.
Janet Are you saying he's agreed—to that?
Celia Not yet, but he will. When I tell him.
Janet You'll never persuade him, love.
Celia I've never persuaded him to do anything. (*Pause. With a cunning expression*) But I've kidded him into doing lots of things. Believe me.

There is the sound of a car off

Janet That sounds like Rupert.
Celia The hunter back to his mate. Stay and listen to him when he comes in. Do you know what he'll say? (*Calling*) "Darling, I'm ho—me!" Who cares?
Janet How do you expect to kid him into it?
Celia There are ways and means. I could forgive him for being a lousy businessman if he wasn't so critical of my house-keeping. He says I'm untidy.

Janet glances about her

Janet How can he say that?
Celia (*shrewdly*) Don't you kid me. I'm untidy because I'm bored, frustrated. I'd have gone places if I'd kept on with my career. He ruined everything when I said I'd marry him.
Janet We'd save ourselves a heap of trouble if once in a while we learned to say "No".

Rupert is heard approaching the front door

Celia Well, I'm saying it now. No to baking and cooking. No to scrubbing and cleaning. And, if necessary, no to something else that'll shake his composure. (*As Rupert reaches the door*) Wait for it—"Darling, I'm home!"

Rupert enters, sees Janet. He merely grunts

Janet Hello, Rupert.
Rupert (*coldly*) How do you do?
Janet (*to Celia*) Don't they let you down? 'Bye.

Janet exits by the front door

Rupert And what, may I ask, did that mean? (*He surveys the room, he is appalled*) Good heavens, woman, look at this room. (*Picking up papers from the floor*) It looks exactly like the Corporation Dump. I've had a hard day at the office—now this. (*Having picked the papers up, he now throws them down again*) God, I'm so tired.

Celia Of course you are, sweetie. You've had a hard day at the office. (*Easing him onto the settee*) It's all too much for you. Let me massage your sinuses. My poor darling.

Rupert (*suspiciously*) Celia, this is me, Rupert, your husband. Remember?

Celia You look so tired.

Rupert (*rising*) All right, what is it?

Celia (*changing her attitude*) I'm bored. In fact, I'm more than that. I'm bored, bored, bored.

Rupert And so am I. (*Moving away*) With you for ever being bored, bored, bored. (*As he passes the ironing-board he burns his hand on the iron which she has not disconnected*) That is typical. What a home to come home to. (*He disconnects the plug*)

Celia Such a charming way to enter a house. Ugh! After being alone all day it's some consolation if I get a cheery greeting.

Rupert (*cunningly*) "Darling, I'm home . . .?"

Celia At least it's friendly.

Rupert I said it yesterday and I distinctly heard you in there—(*he indicates the kitchen*)—say "So what?" If you want to know, I'm as fed up as you are.

Celia Then you're in a very low state.

Rupert I had lunch with my auditors.

Celia Gnawing delicately at a Porterhouse steak.

Rupert Gnawing indelicately at my fingernails. I'm on the point of bankruptcy. Nobody, but nobody, is buying Rupert Johns' soap.

Celia Because nobody's selling them. Rupert Johns One and Two knew how to sell soap.

Rupert Whereas Number Three is a dud. Go on and say it.

Celia It's already been said. Who's contradicting you?

Rupert All the way here I said to myself, "Rupert, don't be disconsolate—the little woman's waiting at home, warm and sympathetic." And what do I get?

He is about to tell her, but she intercedes

Celia What became of the big order you said you'd get last week?

Rupert I didn't get it. (*He picks up a newspaper*)

Celia Why didn't you get it?

Rupert Because he didn't give it to me.

Celia Who didn't?

Rupert Harry Brewster. You've met him. Big flashy fellow. Smells of carbolic.

Celia Why didn't he give you the order?

Rupert Because he prefers carbolic. Please stop asking questions. All I want is peace and quiet.

Celia And food.

He turns to her

Rupert I shouldn't say no to a little something to eat.
Celia It's mince.
Rupert Not again?
Celia Again.
Rupert It is, of course, my favourite dish. But even a gastronomic delight loses a little of its magic on Wednesday when one's already had it on Sunday, Monday and Tuesday.
Celia We didn't have it on Monday.
Rupert Sorry. Silly of me. We had fish fingers.
Celia (*rising*) Are you criticizing my catering?
Rupert Quite frankly I don't think it's any better than my soap. And tastes very similar.

She picks up a vase from an occasional table

Celia You pig!
Rupert (*alarmed*) Celia, your mother gave us that vase.

She replaces it. He sighs

That's better.

She picks up another vase beside the former

Celia, my mother gave us that. Put it down.

She drops the vase on the floor and it breaks

Celia Just as you say, Rupert. (*She moves to the window*)
Rupert You've broken it.
Celia I've hated it for years. I hate you. (*She beats her fists on the curtains*) I'm so bored I could break everything in the house. (*She picks up a clock from the table by the window*)
Rupert Celia, put it down. On the table. Gently.

She puts the clock on the table

That's a good girl.

She now pushes the table—and the clock—over

Have you gone mad? (*He places the clock, which is in pieces, to his ear*)
Celia I hope so. They'd put me away. A room of my own. Someone else to do the cooking.
Rupert That, I admit, would be pleasant.
Celia I hope they do put me away.
Rupert They've got to. Grandfather's clock. (*Reading an inscription on the clock*) "Twenty-five years' President of the Soap Boilers' Guild."
Celia What about me? Ten years' membership of the Women's Guild. Eighteen years in the Mothers' Union and the only clock I've got's an alarm clock. (*From the bookcase she takes a glass object containing a silver medal*)
Rupert Not that.

She threatens to throw it at him

That's the half-mile at school (*He takes it from her*) Four minutes of sheer hell. (*He replaces it*)

Celia I'm a flop. A failure.

Rupert Nonsense. You're nothing of the kind. (*Sniffing*) Isn't there a smell of burning? (*He hurries to the kitchen*)

Rupert exits

Celia Who cares? (*She sits, uncaring*)

Rupert (*calling*) Celia! Celia!

Celia What is it?

Rupert comes back

Rupert Your cooking's on fire.

Celia exits to the kitchen

Rupert looks despondent. We hear crash of pots and pans. He claps his hands together in ironic applause

'Core. 'Core. (*Meaning "Encore"*)

Celia returns

Celia Will scrambled eggs do instead?

Rupert Don't be silly. You never got around to mastering such a delicacy. And you were going to become a *Cordon Bleu* chef. (*Laughing bitterly*) *Cordon bleu!*

Celia *Cordon Bleu* cooks don't have to make do with scrag end of beef and stewing steak every day. They don't have to fight for their housekeeping money. You don't get wild duck on the income of a tame rabbit.

Rupert Are you calling me a rabbit?

She shrugs

You cow.

Celia I will not be called a cow.

Rupert I resent being called a rabbit.

Celia "We'll start small, darling, but in a few years we'll be right up there." The only part of the forecast that came true was the starting small bit. I didn't think it was possible to start at the bottom and go down.

Rupert When you criticize me it's a supreme example of the pot calling the kettle. Since Karen left home, Mrs Beeton, I've had absolutely no home comforts. For one blessed year she attended the Domestic College—my one brief acquaintance with cultured domesticity since I left my mother. Celia, we're almost quarrelling.

She knocks over a vase of flowers

Celia, you have gone stark raving bonkers!

Rupert hurries to the kitchen

Celia Karen did what I should have done. Got a soft, well-paid job in Canada. Lucky her. She gets more money for forty hours' typing than I do for a hundred hours of slavery.

Rupert enters with a floor-cloth. He picks up the vase and mops up the water

Rupert Just look at Grandma's table. (*He kneels*)
Celia I suppose she'll get married, too.
Rupert She was married—for forty years.
Celia Karen.
Rupert Oh, her. Of course she will.
Celia I wonder what she's doing.
Rupert Having a damn good time, I expect. Kids do these days. (*He takes her hand and smiles*) Celia, you're absolutely right. I've let you down. (*He rises*) With a dull thud.
Celia (*dabbing at tears on her cheek*) And I've let you down. I'm the rottenest housekeeper in the world.

He shrugs

Oh yes, I am.

He makes no comment

That's the first statement I've made this week that you haven't contradicted. Do you realize we could become grandparents any time now? Karen could get married and—we haven't got anywhere yet. The only consolation when you're old is to look back with pride on past achievements.
Rupert Damn it, we're not old. *Are* we?
Celia I look a hundred.
Rupert Yes, but you're not. (*He kisses her repentantly*) I don't mean you look old. I mean—damn it, you look younger than Janet.
Celia She's fifty.
Rupert Is she really? Well—surely we can look back on a few happy memories? The early years. Karen's childhood. Measles, chicken-pox, her favourite pony that kicked me in the . . .
Celia Just imagine, she's eighteen. As soon as she'd stopped looking like a suet dumpling—she cleared off to Canada.
Rupert And you're right, we haven't done a damn thing. I'm terribly sorry, Celia.
Celia The first year was fun.
Rupert One out of twenty?
Celia Working together in the office. That's where it all started.
Rupert Mm, funny how things begin. The boss's son and the little typist.

Celia Secretary.
Rupert (*sighing*) You were so pretty in those days. Oh, sorry. (*He kisses her again*) Still are, of course. I remember saying you were the most gorgeous creature I'd ever seen in my life.
Celia I was so ambitious. Getting married killed my career stone dead.
Rupert Darling, I asked you to marry me but I didn't twist your arm and make you say yes.
Celia But I couldn't have a career after that, like you. You didn't carry a baby around inside you for nine months, did you?

He shakes his head and smiles

It wouldn't have furthered your career, if you'd become pregnant, would it?
Rupert On the contrary, I'd have been world-famous. Let's face it, I'm not really astute enough to operate one of those chestnut things at the corner of the street.
Celia And I'm useless in the house. (*Cunningly*) We've gone about things the wrong way.
Rupert How do you mean?
Celia (*very casually*) I ought to be doing what you're doing and vice versa.
Rupert (*laughing*) Swop jobs? That's very funny.
Celia (*seriously*) Except you couldn't do it, of course.
Rupert (*reacting*) How do you mean I couldn't do it?
Celia Running a house isn't as easy as you think. It needs flair.
Rupert Good heavens, woman, I could go through this place in a couple of hours blindfold with one arm in a sling.
Celia But, darling, there's more to it than that. Shopping, cooking, organizing.
Rupert I could play with it.
Celia Oh, no, you couldn't.
Rupert Certainly I could. I'm appalled how much it takes out of you. If I had your job I'd have so much leisure time I'd become cultured. In six months I'd get my golf handicap down to the twenty mark.

Celia appears to be thinking very hard

Celia (*yielding*) Well, I must admit—that dinner party we gave. Trout and almonds. Roast beef. You cooked it all.
Rupert I had to. You'd scalded your fingers boiling an egg.
Celia And when I was ill, you ran the place beautifully. Do you know, darling, you're bringing me round to your point of view.
Rupert I didn't know I had a point of view.
Celia Darling, you've just put the craziest idea in my head. What was the first thing you did when you came home?
Rupert Quarrelled with you.
Celia Yes, but after that?
Rupert I thought I'd walked into a waste-disposal unit.
Celia (*quickly*) But I wasn't like that at the office. Files, papers, contracts. I'd a flair for that just as you've a flair for this.

Rupert That is true. Yes.

Celia Rupert, could we possibly start all over again at the beginning?

Rupert I'm not quite with you.

Celia You were the first to suggest it. Why didn't I think of it? Swopping jobs, I mean.

Rupert Swopping jobs? Are you suggesting you should take over the office whilst I stay here and run the house?

Celia I think it's one of the best ideas you've ever had.

Rupert I don't. I'd be laughed at. Anyway, you were a secretary, not a tycoon. You'd steer the business on the rocks.

Celia Where is it now?

Rupert (*considering*) On the rocks.

Celia So if it is there already, what can we lose?

Rupert (*bemused*) Nothing, I suppose. Celia, the anxieties of that office would get you down. Rags to rags in three generations. It's an old story. Grandfather was a born organizer. Father took after him and married a woman with no brains, and I took after her.

Celia She was a wonderful housekeeper and cook. So are you—marvellous.

Rupert (*coyly*) Don't be silly. Still, you remember I gave a little party for Jim and Brian. The scraggiest chicken you ever saw, but they both said it was the finest *Coq au Vin* they'd ever tasted.

Celia I'll bet it was, too.

Rupert I made that old rooster crow.

Celia Darling . . .

Rupert Yes?

Celia Let's give it a try.

He moves away

Rupert It's quite mad but—(*considering*)—but in the years to come when you're a traffic warden and I'm cleaning out the sewers, at least I've an excuse.

Celia You could blame me.

Rupert (*laughing*) Me a housewife.

Celia Rupert, I bet I'll sell more soap in a week than you've sold in the last two months.

Rupert I haven't sold any. My only big sale this year was to a charming fellow who went bust before I'd time to cash his cheque.

Celia Then, darling, it's obvious, we've nothing to lose and everything to gain. (*As he hesitates*) It's true, isn't it?

Rupert All right—all right. But let's get one thing straight. No more children.

Rupert goes out to the kitchen, he comes back

It was bad enough being a father. I refuse to become a mother.

CURTAIN

Scene 2

The same, several days later

The room is now tidy, everything spick and span. Rupert, the new house-keeper, is more efficient than Celia

When the Curtain rises, the room is empty. Rupert, in the kitchen, is singing cheerfully. The song might be "There is nothing like a man about the house". He walks on quickly, picks up a vase of flowers and goes straight off with it. He is wearing a gaily-coloured apron. Having presumably added water to the vase he comes back quickly, rearranges the flowers, smiles, sighs with self-satisfaction, then picks up the telephone and dials. He sings as he waits

Rupert (*on the telephone*) Hello. Johns here, number twenty-four. . . . That's right, twenty-four Spotted Cow Lane. Is that the butcher? . . . Oh, well now—tomorrow. I shall want some veal. . . . (*Loudly*) Veal. . . . Just a moment. (*He procures and opens a large cookery book*) It says here "Cut shoulder of breast——" . . . You're absolutely right—"shoulder *or* breast, and let soak for twelve hours in cold water with a little lemon juice." (*He puts down the book*) . . . How much? Just a minute. (*He opens the book again*) "Three pounds serves six people." There'll be two of us. Can you work that out? . . . Is it really? How jolly quick of you. It's called—(*reading*)—*Blanquette de Veau*. . . . No, my wife isn't ill, I'm just having a go! By the way, at some stage I've got to—(*reading*)—"remove scum with a perforated spoon." Do you sell perforated spoons? . . . Just meat. . . . Yes, I thought you'd say that. I'll call round later in the morning. By the way, I've heard of a perforated ulcer, but what the hell's a perforated spoon? . . . You presume it's a spoon with holes in it. Thank you very much. (*He replaces the receiver, sings cheerily, opens the book and faces the room reading from it*) "One quart light stock. Black pepper. Carrots. One Spanish onion. Parsley. Thyme. Bay leaf. Celery. Leek. Clove." (*Pause*) "Two egg yolks, twelve button onions, twelve button mushrooms, cream, nutmeg." (*He looks anxious*) The kitchen isn't big enough. (*Reading again*) "Remove bone and fat. Cleanse Casserole. Strain sauce." Think of something simpler. (*He puts the book away*) Rupert, our grasp has exceeded our reach. (*He dials on the telephone*) We must walk before we can . . . Hello? The butcher? . . . Number twenty-four again. I've had second thoughts about the *Veau de Blanquette*. For one thing, I don't know where the hell to get a perforated spoon from, so I'm going to walk before I can run. Have you got a couple of mutton chops? . . . That will do splendidly and I'll pick them up this afternoon. (*He replaces the receiver. He does a few jaunty steps of a Flamenco dance, then reclines on the settee and dials again. He is at ease, prepared for a long casual conversation. On the phone*) Rupert Johns Soaps? . . . I'd like to speak to Mrs Johns. . . . What do you mean, she's engaged? Come off it, nobody's been busy there for years. . . . No, I'm not her husband—she's my wife! Incidentally, who are you? . . . Barry who? . . . Bingley-Brown. We haven't met, I think. . . . Oh, I see, you've replaced Miss Williams. Mrs Johns found her unco-operative, did she really? That's very surprising, I found her most co-operative in every possible way. Well, when there's a lull in her feverish activities, kindly tell her I'm out of coffee and potatoes and to bring some home with her. . . . Oh, I'm so glad she will speak to me. . . . Celia? Who the hell is he? . . . I don't care if you were in the middle of a conference, I can phone my own office, can't I? . . . (*Pause*) Nothing, really. I just wanted a bit of a chat. It's all right for you, I haven't seen a soul since you left the house this morning. . . . Very well, if that's how it is. Sorry I troubled you. Good-bye. (*He snaps down the receiver and rises irritably. Considering*) How dare she sack her? That girl would do anything for Rupert Johns—(*an afterthought*)—and Company.

The telephone rings

(*Answering*) Hello? . . . Oh, it's you. You've rung at a most difficult moment. I'm in the middle of a conference with the grocer's boy. . . . Oh, so that's it. You'll be working late tonight. (*Laughing bitterly*) That's the corniest tale I ever heard. Certainly I've said it myself. Now listen to me, Celia—— (*He replaces the receiver*) Of course I've worked late at the office. That's why I'm bloody suspicious. (*He faces the room, picks up a long feather duster and dabs at cobwebs on the wall*) Good heavens, I bought this brush years ago. It's never been used. (*Moodily he sits in a large chair facing forward. He holds the feather duster at his side, upright like a sentry's rifle*)

There is a gay tapping on the front door. Rat-tata-ta-ta-ta-ta. Robin Nightingale, fortyish, comes in, carrying a bag of house-cleaning equipment. He enters gaily with an extrovert air, sees the feather duster

Rupert reacts but remains still. Robin tip-toes quickly towards the back of the chair, having put down his house-cleaning equipment. He comes up amorously behind chair, suddenly swoops over it, cups Rupert's "bosom" in his hands and kisses him on the cheek. They then face each other and "freeze" in horror. Rupert looks at Robin's hands on his "bosom" and suddenly thrusts them away. He rises quickly

Rupert How dare you, sir?

Robin is aghast

How disgusting.

Robin But I thought . . . (*Gulping*) Who are you?

Rupert That, I should have thought, is for me to ask. Who the hell are you?

Robin Robin.

Rupert Robin?

Robin Yes.

Rupert Hood, Goodfellow, or Redbreast?

Robin Nightingale. Robin Nightingale. I'm from the Arthur Jenkins Clean-Your-Home-Bureau. Personal service. I seem to have made a dreadful mistake. I've come to the wrong house. We do a personal service.

Rupert You certainly do. Was that, may I ask, all a part of it?

Robin I do apologize.

Rupert Heaven knows, I'm broadminded but, quite frankly, I do not like to be kissed. At least, not your variety.

Robin Oh, you've got me wrong. I thought you were a woman.

Rupert Do I look like a woman? (*He discards his apron and duster*) I see what you mean. So you go around cleaning houses, eh? The work seems to have its compensations. (*He decides to be nice about it*) What a marvellous job. Dropping in while hubby's at work and having a bit of slap and tickle with the wife.

Robin Not always, of course. Well, I'd better get along to number twenty-four.

Rupert Where?

Robin Number twenty-four.

Rupert This is number twenty-four.

Robin Oh? Then I'm not at the wrong house after all. (*He laughs, then reacts*) Oh.

Rupert My name's Johns. Are you telling me . . .?

Robin (*hastily*) You see, I have been away for six months. Actually I'm an actor. I only do this when I'm out of a job. I'm just back from a trip to Australia.

Rupert How very nice for the girls Down-Under. (*He moves towards Robin*) My wife must have missed you—(*nastily*)—Robin.

Robin Oh, good Lord no. Not your wife. Your *au pair* girl, Consuelo.

Rupert Oh, her.

Robin Yes, I found her very attractive. (*He gazes around as if looking for her*)

Rupert So did I. That's why she got the push.

Robin I'm sorry to hear that.

Rupert My wife came back early from the Bridge Club and . . . (*Hastily*) We shan't be needing your services any longer. Any of them. As a matter of fact, I do the housework myself.

Robin I wish I could afford to retire.

Rupert Oh, I haven't retired. My wife and I have swopped jobs.

Robin You're pulling my leg.

Rupert No, I'm not. You see, I was no good at business and she was no good in the house so she thought—we thought—would you care for a drink?

Robin Well, thank you very much.

Rupert (*picking up a decanter*) Drop of good stuff. Sit down.

Robin It looks good. (*He sits*)

Rupert I made it myself. Not literally, of course. (*He pours a drink*) Well, I get bored in the afternoons. It's an old recipe handed down from my grandmother. I think you're going to enjoy this. (*Giving Robin the drink*) Try it.

Robin Cheers. (*He drinks*)

Rupert It's made from nettle leaves. Good, eh?

Robin pulls a wry face

Robin Astonishing.

Rupert I'm only allowed to drink whisky. (*He pours himself a whisky and soda*) You seem to have picked yourself a nice job. You're on to something good. Although it appears to have its occupational hazards.

Robin My wife says it's time I went out and got myself a proper job. She's always complaining about money.

Rupert So is mine. At least, she was. Whenever business was good I'd tell her—"This doesn't mean we can live at a higher rate, it means we can almost afford to live at the rate we're already living at." Cheers.

Robin Cheers. Helen—that's my wife—says we can afford to run a car.

Rupert And can't you?

Robin Can anybody? (*Pause*) Of course, we do run one.

Rupert I finally got tired of mine grousing so I finally said: "All right, off you go and do my job. See what sort of a mess you make of it."

Robin And how's she making out?

Rupert It's only her second week. Actually, she's had beginner's luck. Got a damned good order inside a couple of days. And from a hard-hearted bastard who treated me as if I had B.O.

Robin How do you get on with her job?

Rupert With her job. It's a piece of pie. Which reminds me, I'm out of baking powder. The only snag is you're alone too much. In fact, I'm delighted you called. Another drink?

Robin No. No, thanks.

Rupert insists, and refills Robin's glass

Rupert Yes, yes. Good heavens I've got wardrobes full of the stuff. Who'd believe you can make a delicious wine from nettle leaves?

Robin Nobody.

Rupert I think I'll have another, too. (*He pours whisky into his glass*) But perhaps you'd rather have had a drop of Scotch?

Robin (*very politely*) No, no, this is splendid.

Rupert Down the hatch.

Robin drinks, and pulls a face

Robin Do you intend to keep on with it—I mean, the job-swapping?

Rupert Oh, it won't last. I'm being rather cunning. We're on the verge of bankruptcy and you know what bitches even the nicest women can be. She'd have spent the rest of our lives throwing it up at me. Now—(*he smiles*)—she can't.

Robin You mean she'll go bankrupt, not you?

Rupert Exactly.

Robin Then what'll you do?

Rupert notices that Robin wears a badge—A.J.P.S.

Rupert I've no idea. I'll get a job of some sort. What's your firm called? The A.J.P.S. That's worth remembering. Oh, I'll do something. At least I won't spend my declining years being told I went bust.
Robin Suppose she makes a success of it?
Rupert Impossible. Although she's started with a bang. First thing she did was sack my secretary.
Robin Was she no good?
Rupert She was marvellous. Mind you, she was a rotten secretary. (*Considering*) You said, suppose she makes a go of it.
Robin Yes.
Rupert I never thought about that.
Robin Your position would be unbearable.
Rupert Why?
Robin She'd be doling out the housekeeping money. Telling you how much you could have.
Rupert I shouldn't stand for that.
Robin If you swop jobs you swop jobs. She'd hold the purse strings.
Rupert Oh, you don't know her. She's a sweet girl, is Celia.
Robin You said yourself even the nicest women can be bitches.
Rupert You're beginning to get me worried. (*Cheerfully*) Oh, but it won't happen. Just you see, we'll be broke in a couple of months. (*Pleased*) No, everything's all right.
Robin It's the devil and the deep blue sea. You're sunk whatever happens.
Rupert I see what you mean, but if she did pull it off I'd have to make an equal success running the home. And that isn't as easy as you think. All you do is go around with a vacuum cleaner and a tin of floor polish, but can you cook?
Robin Not a sausage.
Rupert There you are, you see. Can you make a *Blanquette de Veau*?

Robin shakes his head

Cubes of veal cut into square shoulders. Spanish onions. Twelve buttons. Fourteen mushrooms. It takes a bit of sticking together, I'll tell you.
Robin Can you do it?
Rupert Certainly I can.
Robin Well done.
Rupert I could get a job any time, anywhere, as a chef.
Robin Oh well, that's fine. Wouldn't do for me, though.
Rupert Why not?
Robin Aren't you afraid it might make you a little . . .?
Rupert A little what?
Robin Effeminate.
Rupert Do I look effeminate to you?
Robin Good heavens, no. But—won't your friends laugh at you?
Rupert That *has* worried me. On the other hand, if she does make a mil-

lion . . . They're all hard up. Who's going to laugh when the chauffeur takes me out shopping?

Robin I must say, though—(*he laughs*)—I thought you looked damn funny in that fancy apron. I had to laugh.

Rupert Did you? I don't think I looked more ridiculous than you did when you discovered I wasn't Consuelo. By the way, change your razor blade. Your chin's like a nailbrush.

Robin Consuelo never complained.

They both laugh

Rupert You found me a little flat-chested, perhaps?

Robin She was well made, wasn't she?

Rupert Yes. Whoever made her knew his job.

Robin Well, I'd better be pushing off.

Rupert I hope we'll meet again. I've enjoyed our little chat. (*Seeing him to the front door*) You get lonely, you know, only talking to the trades-people.

Robin Thank you.

Robin picks up his cleaning equipment

Rupert Oh, I'm so sorry—what a brick. No offence of course. (*He bangs Robin on the shoulder heartily*)

Rupert laughs, but Robin does not

Robin Thanks for the drink.

Rupert Not at all. Call again.

Rupert opens the door

Robin I will. (*As he goes out*) Remember me to Celia.

Robin exits

Rupert, smiling, closes the door

Rupert I will. What a charming fellow. (*Picking up the apron*) Perhaps something a little plainer. (*He frowns*) "Remember me to Celia"? Where's my diary? (*He takes a diary from a drawer in the desk and thumbs the pages*) November. Consuelo got kicked out in—July.

Looking thoughtful, Rupert exits to the kitchen, absent-mindedly putting on his apron

A car approaches and stops. Rupert, preoccupied, does not hear it

Celia enters, carrying a briefcase. She is now very elegant. She puts the briefcase down

Celia (*calling*) Darling, I'm ho—ome!

Rupert enters from the kitchen, like a loving housewife, arms extended, smiling, to greet her

Rupert What a lovely surprise.
Celia Darling.

They embrace

Rupert You said you'd be late and you're early.
Celia I know, but I've only called in on my way out.
Rupert Darling, you look marvellous. Turn around. Gorgeous. How do you mean, on your way out?
Celia We're having dinner with Mr Brewster. I can't get out of it. I'm sorry.
Rupert But that's splendid. Why try to get out of it?
Celia I'm so glad you don't mind.
Rupert (*taking off his apron*) We haven't been out together for ages. I'll get changed. I really ought to have some new clothes. All my shirts are frayed at the edges. Shall I wear my pin-stripe or the blue one?
Celia Darling, you don't understand.
Rupert I do, we're dining out, and I'm delighted.
Celia No, darling. Not you.
Rupert We are dining out, but not me.
Celia I misled you. He invited me, then suggested my new secretary should join us.
Rupert Barry Thingummyjig?
Celia Bingley-Brown.
Rupert That's the fella.
Celia I do hope you're not too disappointed.
Rupert I do hope you're not too serious. Do you mean you're going on the town while Mr Mug sits at home and twiddles his bloody thumbs?
Celia Darling, only to discuss business.
Rupert That's charming.
Celia What can I do about it? I might get a big order. It's very important.
Rupert Isn't our marriage important?
Celia Of course it is.
Rupert You're never at home. Do you know how long it is since you took me out—I mean, since we went out together? Months.
Celia Rupert, it's only ten days since I started working.
Rupert And, come to think of it, we can't afford to entertain Harry Brewster. He nearly ruined me last time. Smoked salmon, pheasant, brandy, two cigars. (*Pause*) Don't tell me he's paying?
Celia Of course. We're his guests.
Rupert Well that is marvellous, the mean sod's sponged off me for years, but you get taken out. Are you sure his mind's on soap?
Celia (*incredulously*) Rupert, you're jealous.
Rupert Don't be absurd.
Celia Anyway, I'll have a chaperon. Barry will be there.
Rupert That makes me feel much better. For ten days Cinderella's seen nothing but these four walls.

Celia They're all I saw for twenty years.

Rupert Oh, yes, and another of your gentlemen friends called to see you today. Robin Skylark. He sent his love.

Celia Who? Oh; Nightingale. Didn't he go to Australia?

Rupert Having whistled a sailor's farewell to the birds in Wagga Wagga, he now wishes it to be known he's roosting on his old perch.

Celia After he left I told the cleaning firm I'd manage for myself. They're quite expensive. Darling, I'll have to go.

Rupert Enjoy yourself.

Celia You're cross.

Rupert I am. Seething.

Celia When you dined out I wasn't invited. What's the difference?

Rupert One major change is that I footed the bill.

Celia I must get ready. (*She opens the outer door, then calls*) Five minutes.

Celia shuts the front door and starts up the stairs. Rupert looks out of the window

Rupert Who's that in a Mercedes-Benz sports car?

Celia Barry.

Rupert They cost about ten thousand pounds.

Celia His family has money. He's only taken this job for the experience.

Rupert What sort of experience?

Celia Don't be silly.

Rupert stares moodily through the window

Rupert He doesn't look to me as if he needs experience. I'd say he's been around plenty.

Celia You're not going to be rude to him, are you?

Rupert I'd say he's a pouff.

Celia Then you've nothing to worry about, have you? But you haven't met, have you?

Barry comes in. A very attractive man, but Rupert does not seem to think so—or does he?

Rupert No.

Celia Barry, this is my husband. Rupert, Barry.

Barry (*charmingly*) How do you do, sir?

Rupert grunts

Rupert I like your car.

Barry Beauty, isn't it? I just traded in my E-type for it. What are you running?

Celia That's a sore point, Barry. I'm using ours for business.

Barry Sorry.

Rupert You will observe my own mode of propulsion leaning against the wall. (*To Celia*) By the way, I need a new bell.

Celia Give Barry a drink whilst I get ready, darling. He likes Scotch.

Rupert We haven't any.
Barry As a matter of fact, sir, I've a bottle of vintage stuff in the car. Dare I suggest—I'll get it.

Barry goes out

Rupert How dare he call me sir? It is a deliberate ploy to make me appear an octogenarian in front of you.
Celia Be nice to him. I was always nice to your secretaries.
Rupert You were bitchy to the lot of them.
Celia Nonsense.
Rupert You soon got rid of Sally Williams.
Celia She was useless. As for typing—with that vulgar bust of hers between her and the machine she could scarcely reach it. Now don't foul up things with Barry because he's . . .

Celia is interrupted by Barry's entrance with a bottle of whisky

Barry Here we are, sir.
Celia Now remember—don't drink too much, darling . . .

Barry hands the bottle of whisky to Rupert

Barry There you are, sir. The best.
Rupert (*pleased, despite himself*) Catto's Rare Old Scottish Highland—twenty years old—I say, we mustn't pollute this. Sit down, sit down. As my grandfather used to say, "Adultery is acceptable in marriage but never with a pure malt whisky." Quite a wag my grandfather.

Celia exits upstairs

Rupert goes to the drinks table for glasses, and holds up his decanter of red wine

As a matter of fact, I've gone into the liquor business myself.
Barry Really?
Rupert Made this on Tuesday. It's damned good. (*He holds up another bottle*) This is a little sweeter—a sort of Sauterne. Care to try it?
Barry (*not too happy*) What a good idea.

Rupert pours the home-made wine into a glass and gives it to Barry

Thank you.
Rupert You don't tread the grapes with your feet yourself, you know, it stains the toenails. I used a pair of old socks.

Rupert pours himself a whisky

Rupert All the best.
Barry All the best, sir.

Barry pulls a wry face as he drinks. Rupert sighs delightedly as he drinks the whisky

Rupert Marvellous.
Barry Yes . . .
Rupert So you're Celia's secretary.
Barry Personal assistant, sir.
Rupert Know anything about soap? Apart from using it, I mean.
Barry Oh, yes. I was with my uncle's firm for ten years. Applebury's.
Rupert Are they your uncle? But they're big. Why did you leave them?
Barry I want to branch out on my own. As a matter of fact, I've fifty thousand pounds I'd like to invest. I've been looking for a smallish established business I could invest in. I've already discussed it with Celia.
Rupert You mean—buy a share in our set-up?
Barry I've thought it might be to our mutual interest.
Rupert You don't say so . . .
Barry Your company needs capital to build it up.
Rupert One can always utilize extra capital. I say, you're not really enjoying that, are you?
Barry It's perhaps a little sweet.
Rupert I rather overdid the sugar. No, no, give it to me. (*He takes the glass from him, pours him a whisky*) Fifty thousand, eh? Yes, that might indeed be to our mutual interest.
Barry Celia likes the idea.
Rupert So do I. (*Carefully*) Mind you, I shouldn't move lightly into a partnership. Especially just now when things are going so well.
Barry Your last year's figures weren't very good, were they?
Rupert You've seen the books?

Barry nods

Rising costs, new machinery . . .
Barry (*raising his eyebrows*) New machinery?
Rupert My secretary's typewriter. You did say fifty thousand pounds, didn't you?

Barry nods

It's true last year's figures weren't very good, but you can't pick out one bad year, can you?
Barry I've seen your figures over the last ten years, Mr Johns. Frankly, I can't pick out one good one.
Rupert Nineteen fifty-eight was rather exciting.
Barry I didn't go so far back.
Rupert Oh, wonderful year. Showed a profit.

Celia comes down the stairs

Celia That didn't take long, did it?
Rupert Darling, don't interrupt. (*To Barry, very casually*) I don't want to raise your hopes too high but we might lunch together sometime in the future and discuss it. (*Eagerly*) Tomorrow?

Celia Rupert, darling . . .
Rupert (*to Barry*) I've been taking a few days off—sort of sabbatical. I see it's time I was back.
Barry Back, sir?
Rupert The old helm, you know.
Barry But I understood . . .
Rupert Yes?
Barry That Celia—Mrs Johns—was running the business.
Celia Barry, dear, wait outside in the car. I'd like a word with my husband before we go.
Barry See you later, sir.
Rupert Yes indeed. Give me a ring some time. To save time, I'll ring you.

Barry goes out

Celia Darling, I don't know how to say this, but Barry's suggested buying a partnership in the business.
Rupert I know that, and if you hadn't interrupted . . .
Celia But only on one condition.
Rupert I'll make the conditions. I'm prepared to consider his application, and if it suits me . . .

She helps him into a chair

Celia The condition is—(*she pauses*)—that you never go near the office again.

Pause. Rupert rises

Ever.
Rupert How the hell can I run things if I don't go near the office?
Celia (*helping him back into the chair*) You can't. That's the condition. Things are going so much better since I took over. Barry thinks it should stay that way.
Rupert He has a nerve.
Celia He knows we're practically bankrupt and, to be brutally frank, darling, he blames you. He thinks I'll succeed where you failed.
Rupert (*rising*) How bloody dare he? (*He goes to the outer door, opens it, and calls sternly*) Mr Brown. If you please.
Celia (*quietly*) Rupert—quickly and quietly—before he gets here.
Rupert I'll cut him down to size. Just watch.
Celia On Monday the bank manager sent for me. He insists our overdraft be reduced at once. On Tuesday we received a summons to appear in the County Court for non-payment of rates. On Wednesday Tickford's sent their account for the fourth time, plus a rude letter withdrawing our credit. On Thursday your Accountant rang up to say we owe a full year's tax and the Ministry is asking why none of the workers' cards has been stamped. Today . . .

Barry knocks on the door and enters

Barry You called me, sir?
Rupert Did I? Oh, I'll just get the cork for you. The bottle of Scotch. (*With an effort*) Did I thank you?
Barry My pleasure, sir.
Rupert Oh, thank you.
Celia (*with a sigh*) See you later, darling.
Rupert Have a good time.

They kiss

Celia Ready, Barry?
Barry Yes, indeed. Good-bye, sir.
Celia 'Bye, darling.

Rupert "smiles" and waves "pleasantly"

Celia and Barry exit, leaving the front door ajar

Rupert hurries to the window

Rupert Spoiled brat. Ruined by indulgent parents. Doesn't know what it is to be self-made like me. (*Pacing the floor*) When you've achieved it by your own efforts you can be proud of yourself. (*He smiles and waves through the window*)

The car drives away

His manners are too oily for my liking. You called, sir? My pleasure, sir. Good-bye, sir. If he isn't one of those he's one of the others, which is worse. You'll repay watching, my lad. My fault business wasn't good. I worked my fingers to the bone in that office and now—(*he gestures*)—kicked out if you like. And by whom? My own wife and a bloke who's still wet behind the ears . . . I should have clouted him across one of them. Wish I had. With all that financial backing she's sure to succeed. We shan't go bankrupt after all. How ghastly. I'll stay here till I'm doddery. Nothing but these four walls. I'll start talking to myself, and that'll be the end . . . Lux, Daz, Fairy Snow, Threepence off. I'll go to pieces.

There is a knock on the front door. Rupert paces up and down. The knock is repeated

I won't see a single bloody soul.

The door is opened and Inga Peterson enters shyly. She is a very beautiful Scandinavian

Rupert does not see her

Inga (*suddenly, nervously, quickly*) Hello. I'm Inga Peterson.

He turns in surprise

Front Stage

We're your new neighbours. Mrs Johns told me to drop in any time if I feel lonely. (*She sobs. Her voice rises to a tearful crescendo*) I feel lonely.

He stares at her

Rupert So do I.
Inga My husband's left me.
Rupert So has mine.
Inga He's taken his secretary out to dinner and he says I can't go. We haven't been out together for years.
Rupert Neither have we.
Inga I'm so lonely.
Rupert So am I.

She becomes more tearful. With a handkerchief he dabs away the tears from her eyes. His arm goes about her shoulder. The telephone rings but they ignore it. They stand in the middle of the room, his arm about her, her head on his shoulder. Having dabbed at her eyes with his handkerchief he—with considerable emotion—blows his nose as—

the CURTAIN *falls*

SCENE 3

The same. 7 p.m., four weeks later

Rupert, Janet, Inga and Robin are seated round a card-table, playing. Rupert, on the settee, is jacketless, relaxed, content. The "quarrels" between him and Robin are jocular, each laughing at his own joke. They play their cards

Janet I've no luck with cards.
Rupert That, Janet, dear, is not correct. You've more luck than I have, but I happen to possess a super-abundance of skill. My trick, thank you, I have the Ace.
Janet You always have.
Inga So you don't need a great deal of skill, Rupert.
Robin Oh, yes, he does. When he shuffles the cards . . .
Rupert I'm not sure I like that.
Robin I'm not sure I do.
Rupert Are you suggesting that I'd stoop to cheating?
Robin Are you suggesting that you wouldn't?
Rupert Well, really.
Robin I've observed with interest that good cards find their way into your hand when they've recently passed through your fingers in the shuffle.
Rupert If I thought you were serious I should ask you to step outside.
Robin I am serious.
Rupert Then step outside. (*He caresses Inga and Janet*) I'll stay here with

the girls. (*He puts down a card*) Ace of Clubs. Solo. (*To Inga, sweetly*) That's another fourpence you owe me. It'll do later. ("*Nastily*" *to Robin*) Fourpence, please.

Robin You're losing your touch. You only had four aces that time.

They pay out their losses, Rupert happily receives it. The telephone rings

Inga I say, it must be six o'clock. David's furious if dinner isn't on the table at seven.

Rupert (*on the telephone*) Rupert Johns. Who?

Robin (*to Inga*) He'll be livid tonight. It's seven now. (*He deals*)

Inga It isn't!

Rupert (*on the telephone*) Yes, she is. We're playing cards. I'm winning. I just had two aces, King, Queen, Jack of Clubs, and . . . Seven o'clock? Is it really? Doesn't time fly as you get older. I'll tell her. (*He replaces the receiver, sits, picks up the cards which Robin has dealt*)

Inga
Janet } (*speaking together*) Who was it?

Rupert Your husband. Who dealt this lot? (*To Robin*) You?

Janet Was it Henry?

Rupert I've no idea.

Inga Who telephoned, Rupert?

Rupert I didn't ask. A voice said "Is my wife there, I'm bloody hungry."

Janet It sounds like Henry. We've been here since half past two.

Inga I haven't been shopping yet.

Rupert He probably had a damn good lunch on his expense account. Marvellous how they fiddle the Inland Revenue. It's disgusting.

Janet We'll play this hand.

Inga He's getting as fat as a pig, anyway.

Rupert So is Celia. I look after her too well. Since I took over she's put on half a stone.

Robin Dare I suggest we continue our game? I happen to have a decent hand for once.

Rupert Naturally. You dealt, didn't you?

The telephone bell rings

Excuse me. (*He goes to the telephone, taking his cards*) Rupert Johns. (*To Robin*) You did a marvellous job on this lot. (*To the phone*) Is who there?

Robin Solo.

Rupert Pass. (*To the phone*) I know it's seven o'clock. I'm hungry too. Excuse me. (*He examines his cards*)

Inga Pass.

Janet Pass.

Rupert (*to the phone; casually*) It's seven o'clock, you're hungry and what the hell does she think she's doing. I'll tell her. (*He returns to the table*)

They play the cards

Robin You've put a trump on my Ace.

Rupert Because I can't think of anything better to do with it. Can you?
Robin Are you sure you haven't any Spades?
Rupert You ought to know. You dealt. (*He enjoys himself*) I say, this is a marvellous way to spend an afternoon. When Celia was at home she hated the Bridge Club. (*He plays a card*) I don't know why.
Robin Every time I play a card you trump it.
Rupert I know. Isn't it fun?
Robin You must have some Spades.
Rupert Want to look?
Robin Yes, I do.
Rupert Fourpence?
Robin Agreed.

Rupert shows his cards

My God, he hasn't.
Rupert Fourpence, please. The rest are mine. (*He plays his last card*) You're down. That's eightpence to me and fourpence each to the girls. Bad luck, Robin. You do play so badly, don't you?

Robin pays up. Inga and Janet rise and prepare to leave

Robin I suppose I'd better trot along, too. (*To Rupert, smiling*) You'd better put your pinny on, old boy. Celia'll be home soon hungry as a hunter. (*He laughs*)
Rupert There's no need to be sarcastic.

Inga and Janet are ready to leave

Janet 'Bye.

Rupert pecks her cheek briefly

Inga I *have* enjoyed it.
Rupert Next Tuesday? Same time? (*He kisses her with great pleasure*)
Janet Inga . . .
Inga Right. 'Bye.

Rupert kisses Inga again, and sighs

Inga and Janet go

Robin By the way, how's Celia managing with your job?
Rupert Extremely well. If you must know, it's proved a damn good arrangement.
Robin Yes—wouldn't do for me, of course. I say, Inga's a bit of all right.
Rupert Yes, she is, isn't she?
Robin Does Celia know about her? I mean—dropping in on you when she's lonely?
Rupert Of course she knows.
Robin How do you know she knows?
Rupert Because two minutes after Inga arrives so does Janet. Celia's obviously told her to keep an eye on us.

Robin Women are cunning. Does she work late at the office?
Rupert Janet or Inga?
Robin Celia.
Rupert Occasionally.
Robin Mm. Rupert—I'm not sure I should tell you this but—(*hesitating*)—I hate gossip.
Rupert So do I. What have you heard? (*He smiles, then scowls*) Do you mean about me and Inga?
Robin (*quickly*) What could I hear about you and Inga?
Rupert Nothing, of course.
Robin No, I mean a chap called Brewster. Frankly, I wouldn't trust him a yard—near women, I mean. They say he's got his sights on Celia.
Rupert I trust her implicitly.
Robin Of course you do, but he's a shocker.
Rupert He puts a lot of business in her way.
Robin Did he put a lot of business in your way?
Rupert Certainly. (*He is obviously not being truthful*) He was my best customer and a very generous friend.
Robin Oh, well, perhaps he's genuine for once. They go to the Hole-in-the-Wall at six o'clock. Brewster breathing over one shoulder and Barry Bingley-What's-his-name over the other. No doubt she can look after herself, but they're a fine pair, they are.
Rupert Wouldn't do for you . . .
Rogin I have a jealous streak. We're all made differently. (*He moves towards the front door*)
Rupert No, Robin, we're all made the same. Some of us possess finer qualities than others, that's all.

A car is heard approaching

Is that Celia?
Robin (*near the window*) Yes. See you Tuesday, Rupert.

Robin goes out

Rupert "thinks"

Celia enters with her briefcase

Celia Hello, darling.
Rupert Hello.

She puts down her briefcase, kisses Rupert on his cheek, then collapses into a chair

Celia God, I'm tired.
Rupert Poor darling.
Celia Pour me a drink, darling.
Rupert Sherry, darling?
Celia Scotch, darling.

Rupert Have we any Scotch?
Celia I brought a bottle yesterday. Barry gets it from his father wholesale.
Rupert Barry? Oh, yes. (*He gets a bottle, pours drinks*) Had a busy day, darling?
Celia Hell let loose. What's for dinner? I'm as hungry as a hunter.
Rupert Aren't we dining out? I thought we'd trot along to the Chanticleer.
Celia It's far too expensive.
Rupert Business is good, isn't it?
Celia Of course, but we aren't in the millionaire class yet.
Rupert I can't remember when I last ate a meal somebody else had cooked. I only had a sandwich for lunch. I suppose you went to the Hole-in-the-Wall?
Celia We only had salad and a snack.
Rupert We?
Celia Yes.
Rupert (*casually*) Who's we, darling?
Celia Barry and I.

He gives her the drink

Rupert Wasn't Brewster there? (*He picks up his own drink*)
Celia As a matter of fact, yes, he did join us.
Rupert The three of you . . .?
Celia (*rising*) Yes, darling. (*She goes to him, smiles*) Oh, come on. We *will* go out to dinner. Blow the expense.

They kiss

Let's celebrate.
Rupert Celebrate what, darling?
Celia Today Harry gave me a five thousand pound order. Congratulate me.
Rupert *Did* he? By Jove.
Celia Darling, I think I've got what it takes.
Rupert He seems to think so. Tell me—as you're selling the identical soap I was selling, why is he buying from you when he didn't buy from me? What have you got that I haven't?
Celia He says he likes my approach. Admires positive women. His wife's a bit of a mouse.
Rupert And according to my information he's a bit of a rat. I'm the last man in the world to be influenced by gossip—too big for that sort of thing—but I think you should be careful.
Celia What *do* you mean?
Rupert People are talking, darling. They say you're seeing too much of him.
Celia Who's talking?
Rupert People—people.
Celia People?
Rupert Robin says . . .

Celia Robin. He should talk.
Rupert Why?
Celia He's jealous.
Rupert Of you?
Celia He's always made passes at me. Of course he's jealous.
Rupert He isn't the one that's jealous. I'm the one that's jealous.
Celia Oh! So you're too big to be influenced by gossip.
Rupert I mean I'm the one who has a right to be jealous. Only, of course, I'm not jealous. I laughed in his face. He says he wouldn't stand for Bingley-Brown either.
Celia Oh, so you're jealous of him as well.
Rupert I didn't say so.
Celia But you are.
Rupert Yes. No. I merely resent hearing gossip about you.
Celia If you were any kind of a man you'd have punched his nose.
Rupert I don't see why you can't have a female secretary. I did.
Celia You certainly did. A whole string of tarts with inflated bosoms.
Rupert Please don't be vulgar.
Celia Darling, we're not quarrelling, are we?
Rupert Yes, we are.
Celia I mean, we mustn't. (*She takes his hand*) You're not unhappy at home, are you?
Rupert I get a little bored sometimes.
Celia You enjoy your Tuesday card game, don't you?
Rupert Yes.
Celia And Inga drops in to see you quite regularly, doesn't she?
Rupert Yes. (*Quickly*) *And* Janet.
Celia Come on, let's get ready. I'll ring up and book a table. It'll be nice to have really *Cordon Bleu* food for a change.
Rupert How do you mean, it'll be nice? We eat well at home, don't we?
Celia Of course, darling.
Rupert I haven't got a bloody staff of waiters to help me, you know. I do it all myself on a very tight budget. And, that reminds me, I can't manage on the money I'm getting. I shall have to have more.
Celia I'm giving you as much as you gave me.
Rupert The cost of living's gone up since then. Besides, we're eating better than when you were doing it.
Celia We're spending too much already. Your trouble is you don't know how to do the buying. You just breeze up to the counter, flash your eyes at the girls and say "I'll take this, that and the other". If you'd look more at the prices and less at girls, your money would go a lot farther.
Rupert I flash my eyes at shop assistants?
Celia You always have.
Rupert You make it sound so coarse. As if I've got a flash bulb behind them switching them on and off. Now who's jealous?
Celia If I were of a jealous nature I could find someone much nearer home to be jealous of.

Rupert For example?

Celia Well, darling, people are talking about you, too.

Rupert Which people?

Celia People, people.

Rupert People?

Celia Janet says——

Rupert Ha, ha! Janet . . .

Celia She says Inga's virtually moved in.

Rupert So has Janet. She's round here so fast it's as if she was on the end of a piece of elastic. And you've put her up to it.

Celia Darling, if you don't mind gossip, I don't. But it might reach her husband's ears.

Rupert He neglects her. I know how she feels.

Celia (*picking up the phone and dialling*) You and I both know it's innocent, darling, but he doesn't know you as well as we do. (*On the phone*) The Chanticleer? . . . May I reserve a table for two? . . . Tonight. . . . I know I've left it late but this is Celia Johns. . . . You can? About eight-fifteen. Thank you so much. (*She replaces the receiver*) They were fully booked, but they'll find a table for us.

Rupert Why?

Celia As a special favour.

Rupert They don't know us.

Celia They know me, darling. Harry, Barry and I were there last week.

Rupert Harry, Barry and I. At the Chanticleer. Inga, Janet and I have tea and biscuits in the kitchen.

Celia Darling, there was none of this terrible atmosphere when *you* went out to work.

Rupert I'd no idea of the temptations surrounding you at home.

Celia You were quite happy with the temptations that surrounded you at the office.

Rupert At least we never got ourselves talked about. I trusted you implicitly.

Celia I didn't trust you.

Rupert Janet's proof of that. Anyway, we're changing the subject. Either my budget rises or my services suffer. As you wish.

Celia begins to giggle

I'm serious, Celia.

Celia I know you are. I'm sorry. (*She goes to him, takes his arm*) You looked so funny, folding your arms and holding out for your rights. Rupert, we've quarrelled ever since I came home. We can't go on like this.

Rupert I agree. I slave all day to make the place nice and cosy for when you come home, and what do I get? Grumbles. Meanness. Complaints.

Celia I've had a hard day at the office, darling. I'm so exhausted I could cry. And what do I get?

Rupert laughs

Now what?

Rupert That's exactly what I used to say to you.

Celia And you're behaving as I used to.

Rupert I know.

They kiss

Celia Oh come on. You're not really unhappy at home, are you?

Rupert No. Let's have another drink. (*He refills the glasses*) I haven't seen you look so relaxed since Karen left home. You must admit I'm doing a good job.

Celia I do. But so am I, darling.

Rupert Of course you are.

Celia It *is* working out well, isn't it? You enjoy all the things I hated.

Rupert I've arranged to join the Painting Class. Oh, and next week we're going to the New Arts Centre. They've asked us to join the Drama Club.

Celia Us?

Rupert Inga and I. And Janet. She'll be there—no doubt.

Celia I'll see to that.

They laugh

So we continue then? All right?

Rupert Right.

Celia I'll admit I'm loving every minute of it.

Rupert (*kisses her*) Do you realize we're happier than we've been for ages?

Celia I know.

They embrace

Karen enters through the front door. She is an attractive twenty-year-old

Karen Surprise, surprise. Hello.

They all embrace

Rupert Karen. Why didn't you tell us you were coming?

Karen I didn't dare.

Celia Didn't dare?

Karen I was in Canada this morning. Isn't it marvellous?

Rupert What do you mean, you daren't tell us?

Karen I'd thought of going to Aunt Margaret's.

Celia What? Instead of here? This is your home.

Karen Daddy, I've a taxi outside. Help me with my things. (*To Celia, indicating the drink*) Can I have a drink?

Rupert and Karen go out through the front door, his arm about her

Celia, smiling, pours a drink for Karen

After a moment, Karen enters with luggage

(*As she enters*) How lovely to see you again.

Celia I thought Daddy was bringing the luggage in?

Karen He's paying the taxi driver.

Karen embraces Celia

Rupert enters. In each hand he carries a carry-cot. He appears dazed

Celia sees him over Karen's shoulder

Celia What have you got there?

Rupert (*looking at them*) Kids.

Celia What?

Karen plays the rest of the scene in an elusive manner, vaguely, absent-mindedly

Karen Twins. (*Changing the subject*) Oh, it's nice to be back. As if nothing's ever happened.

Rupert Not to me it doesn't. I'd say something *has* happened.

Celia Whose are they?

Karen (*in a small voice*) Mine. (*Brightly, looking at a picture on the wall*) I love that painting. Was it expensive?

Celia Darling, shouldn't we have been told?

Karen (*vaguely*) Told?

Celia About this. These.

Karen Yes, you should. (*She nods gravely*) Yes. I didn't quite know how to tell you. (*Brightly*) But you know how you always say you like surprises. (*She sits*)

There is silence. Her brightness ends in a rather sickly smile. She gestures vaguely. Rupert suddenly revives

Rupert There are surprises and surprises. We weren't even invited to the wedding. We didn't even hear about the wedding.

Karen No . . .

Celia Where is your husband?

Rupert Where was the wedding?

Celia And Karen—where's your wedding ring?

Karen (*rising*) Mummy. (*Brightly*) May I have my drink?

Celia (*anxiously*) Darling, what have you done?

Rupert now explodes

Rupert I'll tell you what she's done. She has come home with a couple of——

Karen (*shocked*) Daddy, please!

Celia closes her eyes

Celia (*to Rupert*) Not in front of your grandchildren.

Rupert Grandchildren?

They are amazed to discover they are suddenly grandparents, as—

the CURTAIN *falls*

ACT II

Scene 1

The same. 2 p.m., some days later

The room is no longer as neat and tidy as it was. Children's toys, etc. are lying around. Rupert is busy at the ironing-board. Ash from his cigarette drops on to the clothes he is ironing. He blows it off. Karen enters from the kitchen, carrying a shopping basket. She is neat and relaxed, whereas Rupert is harassed

Karen I'm going shopping. I've left your grandchildren out there in the sun. Keep an eye on them.

He ignores her

I need some more tins of baby food. Daddy, you can't sulk forever.

Rupert We believed in breast feeding.

Karen That's all right if you've got the equipment—I didn't want them to starve.

Rupert It's little more than a year since you left home with your head held high.

Karen Fourteen months. And it's still high.

Rupert I hope you're ashamed of yourself.

Karen Yes, Daddy, but you know I'm not.

Rupert Fourteen months ago we saw you off in high glee. A nice girl. Travelling alone. And now . . .

Karen There are three of us.

Rupert How did it happen? That's what I'd like to know.

Karen Well, Daddy, there are these birds and these bees.

Rupert I flatter myself on my sense of humour, but I see nothing funny —or clever—in allowing some dissolute Canadian to land you—and me—in this predicament.

Karen Rod isn't dissolute and I'm not in a predicament.

Rupert He should be ironing these damned things—not me. I used to look forward to Tuesday so much. You've ruined everything.

Karen I wasn't to know you and Mummy had changed sex, was I?

Rupert Don't be flippant. We'd have been better off if you and your lousy lover had changed sex, then *his* father would have been in the cart.

Karen Rod isn't a lousy lover. Oh, believe me.

Rupert Karen, please! I've no time for all this sloppy modish thinking. I suppose you think marriage is *passé bourgeois* nonsense?

Karen Not at all. I'm very old-fashioned about it. So is Rod. We both believe in the sanctity of marriage. For ever and ever. Daddy, we really do.

Rupert Then why the hell aren't you married?

Karen We're going to be just as soon as Rod gets his divorce.

Rupert Do you mean he's already married?

Karen I thought I told you so.

Rupert Not me, no. It must have been someone else.

Karen I told Mummy. (*Suddenly*) We decided not to tell you straight away, in case you worried about it.

Rupert Worried? Over little things like—(*he points*)—those?

Karen Mummy promised not to tell you. I said I'd rather you learned gradually.

Rupert So there was a conspiracy.

Karen I thought you would be a bit stuffy. I'm so glad you're taking it well. Rod's wife was deceiving him and so he's divorcing her.

Rupert Let's see if I've got it right. He's prepared to uphold the sanctity of marriage, for ever and ever, as soon as he gets a divorce.

Karen Yes. And as soon as it's finalized he's coming to England to marry me. Don't worry, Daddy. We'll make an honest man of you yet.

Rupert I'm ashamed to show my face in the village.

Karen That's all right. I'll do all the shopping. Can I get anything for you?

Rupert Yes, some hand lotion—my once magnolia smooth hands are now as rough as a Scottish thistle.

Karen It's funny, I thought Mummy'd be difficult, not you. I thought you'd take it in your stride.

Rupert Your mother isn't doing the ironing, is she? She doesn't have to face the neighbours. "I hear your daughter's back home with two lovely children. We're dying to meet her husband." What do I say? "She isn't married, but it's all right—the father is." That I suppose, makes it half-respectable.

Karen You'll love him when you meet him.

Rupert If I meet him, which I doubt very much, the only pleasure I shall derive will be punching him on the nose. Taking advantage of a visitor to the country.

Karen Taking advantage—but you and Mummy had a whirlwind romance.

Rupert I wasn't standing at Tilbury Docks lecherously awaiting the arrival of foreign immigrants.

Karen I'd reached the age of consent, you know.

Rupert Reaching the age of consent doesn't mean you *have* to consent.

Karen What's the use of having the vote, if you don't exercise it?

Rupert In that case you should have selected your candidate more carefully.

Karen I'm sorry you disapprove.

Rupert "Disapprove" is far from being a fulsome definition of how I feel about it.

Karen I am sorry. For you, I mean.

Rupert But not for yourself?

Karen I love him.

Rupert No sense of shame.

Karen I'm sorry I've let the side down. After all, we only did what you and Mummy did.

Rupert With one exciting difference. You were ahead of the marriage ceremony.

Karen Weren't you?

He looks thoughtfully at her

I shouldn't have asked that. I'm sorry if I've embarrassed you. (*She goes to the outer door*)

Rupert I always made a point of being . . .

Karen Careful? (*She smiles*) Daddy, you've been a womanizer all your life. I was always so proud of you. Even at school the girls used to say "He's so gorgeous," and I loved it.

Rupert At school? (*He is pleased*)

Karen Yes.

Rupert Did they really?

Karen Miss Jackson, the headmistress, blushed like a rose when you came along.

Rupert Nonsense.

Karen You know she did. Women have always fallen for you. It was nice for me having a father like that. (*As she goes towards the door*) I guess you've laid hundreds.

Rupert (*shocked*) Karen!

Karen smiles, throws a kiss and goes out

(*To himself*) Laid hundreds . . . ? A gross exaggeration, what a charming thought . . . (*He picks up his iron, smiling, touches the bottom of the iron, which is hot, irons*)

Robin enters from the outer door, carrying a peg-basket, napkins over one arm, a peg in his mouth. He murmurs inaudibly

Rupert turns brightly

Inga, darling . . . Oh, it's you.

Robin takes the peg from his mouth

Robin These were dry, so I've brought them in. What the hell are you doing?

Rupert What do I look as if I'm doing?

Robin You look more like a mother than a grandfather.

Rupert The only reason I do this is because Karen's as sloppy in the house as her mother. If I leave it to her the kids will have sore bottoms. Make yourself useful.

Robin (*helping*) You can buy disposable napkins nowadays.

Rupert What I await is the invention of disposable infants. The ideal number of children in a family is none. By the way, he's married.

Robin Who is?

Rupert (*holding up a napkin*) The blighter who brought these damned things into my life.
Robin That's not so good.
Rupert She says he's trying to get a divorce. That's the hoariest gag in the Seducer's Handbook. Used it myself dozens of times.
Robin I suppose there'll be no more card sessions with the girls?
Rupert No painting classes, either. Nothing but nappies and howling kids.

Robin puts down the nappies

Robin (*casually*) We'll just have to have them at my place, that's all.
Rupert Then your wife would know you weren't at work. She doesn't know you take a holiday every Tuesday afternoon, does she?
Robin As a matter of fact, she won't be home on Tuesdays. (*Pause*) or Wednesdays. In fact, she won't be there at all now.
Rupert She hasn't left you?

Robin hesitates awkwardly

I'm terribly sorry. What's happened?
Robin (*angrily*) If you want to know, it's all your bloody fault.
Rupert I beg your pardon?
Robin And so you should.
Rupert I've never even met your wife.
Robin You don't have to. You perform your wonders by remote control.
Rupert What are you talking about?
Robin She's got a job.
Rupert Helen?
Robin Yes, damn it.
Rupert Is that so bad?
Robin Of course it is. Ghastly.
Rupert Won't it subsidize your income?
Robin Which income?
Rupert The Arthur how's your father, clean your thing bureau.
Robin I was sacked on Friday and on Saturday Helen went out and got herself a job. Fellow she used to work for before we got married. He's always wanted her back. Now he's got her. He's paying her twice as much as I was earning.
Rupert Then you're better off.
Robin I enjoyed my career. It had the spice and element of adventure.
Rupert You mean hiding in wardrobes? (*He laughs*)
Robin And it's all your fault. Look at you, ironing nappies. Doing the washing. Slowly but surely developing into an old Mary Ann.
Rupert What a rotten thing to say.
Robin Helen and I used to giggle about you. I'd go home and say "Poor old Rupert's custards went wrong. The milk boiled over." Or "Poor old Rupert's having trouble with his new kitchen sink. No doubt Celia will put it right when she comes home from work." (*He laughs*)
Rupert I thought we were friends.
Robin That's why I found it rather sad to watch your deterioration. Now

I've got the sack, Helen's got a good job, and . . . (*He paces up and down*) The only reason I don't kick you up the backside is that you've got bigger feet than I have.

Rupert What have I got to . . . ? Just a minute. Are you telling me . . . ?

Robin Yes, damn it.

Rupert You mean you and Helen . . . ?

Robin Yes, I do.

Rupert She's going out to work, and you're . . . (*He laughs*)

Robin The bloody housewife. She says if you can do it I can. Once a thing like this starts there's no knowing where it'll stop. Revolutions start in cellars—this was hatched in your kitchen.

Rupert I see what you mean.

Robin Man should dominate. You know what happened when the Amazons took over.

Rupert No.

Robin I've forgotten myself, but it wasn't good. The whole trend of life today encourages this sort of thing. Girls in trousers, men with long hair. But instead of stopping it, you've given it a bloody big push forward.

Rupert I'm sorry.

Robin If the card sessions continue they'll have to be at my place. By the way, you might lend me one of your books. (*He goes towards the bookcase*) I forget what it's called. This. (*He sheepishly gives Rupert a book*)

Rupert (*reading*) *One hundred fish dishes*—by Monica Ling.

Robin (*selecting another book*) And this, if you can spare it. (*Awkwardly*) You said you found it useful.

Rupert (*reading the title*) *Encyclopaedia of European Cuisine.* Of course you can borrow it. It's a bit advanced, though. Isn't this more in your line? (*He hands a slim volume to Robin*)

Robin *Simple Cooking for Beginners.* Perhaps you're right. Thanks.

Rupert By the way, it's early-closing day. Have you done your shopping?

Robin I got a few things. (*He goes out and returns with a large shopping basket, a large eel-like fish is hanging over the edge of it*)

Rupert What the devil's that?

Robin Isn't it obvious?

Rupert It's a conger eel. I never saw anything so horrible in my life. You should be very careful buying fish. Be sure it's fresh.

Rupert holds up the fish. Robin smells it

Robin It smells fresh enough to me.

Rupert It doesn't smell fresh, it smells high. The eyes should be bright. Those aren't bright, they're glazed. (*He puts it back in the basket*) Anyway, no-one eats those things.

Robin What do they do with them?

Rupert (*glancing into the book*) Observe them through plate glass windows, the thicker the better, in aquariums. I wouldn't feed that to a cat. Good lord, they do eat them.

Robin What's it say?

Rupert According to Monica they stew them in beer in Hamburg.
Robin I like the sound of that.
Rupert (*reading*) "Take eels as required"—you've only got one—"and add a pint of beer. Serve very hot. Or, if preferred, serve very cold." I should serve it cold, as a fertilizer. What else have you bought?

They examine the basket: tins and packet foods

Robin Beans, mashed potatoes, rice pudding.
Rupert And a sea-serpent. You're smart. A week of this and your wife will throw in the sponge.
Robin You're jealous.
Rupert Of whom?
Robin You think you're the only one who can cook. I'm not a fool, you know.
Rupert Robin, if you're going to change places with Helen, do it properly. Taking over the kitchen is the one time in a man's life when he has the opportunity to eat well. Women can't cook. What's this? Beans? I never knew a time when my father didn't suffer from dyspepsia. There is a time in the life-cycle of a bean when it isn't confined to a tin. Once it climbed joyously, laughing and carefree, up bamboo poles. Tomorrow I will take you shopping and open your eyes to a rarity which can still be unearthed if sought diligently. (*Picking up another tin*) And I don't mean rice pudding. Fresh food. (*He drops the tins contemptuously into the basket*)
Robin You seem to know a lot.
Rupert If we have failed in one department we must succeed in another. Face facts, Robin. If we don't achieve excellence in any damn direction at all, we've no *raison d'être*.
Robin I don't want a *raison d'être*. Just an easy going-on. I'm a lotus-eater.
Rupert (*pointing to the basket*) Then at least eat fresh lotuses. You don't seem to have a vocation.
Robin I certainly haven't a vocation for training laughing beans up poles or picking my own rice in a paddy field.

Rupert shakes his head sadly. Babies begin to cry upstairs

Or ironing another man's nappies.
Rupert She said they'd stay asleep until she got back. (*He goes towards the stairs*)
Robin I'll see you later.
Rupert You're not going, are you? Damn it, there are two of them.
Robin I also have no vocation as a nanny.
Rupert What a friend you are.

Rupert exits upstairs

Robin thoughtfully looks at his tins and the conger eel

Robin (*holding up the fish to eye-level*) They're as bright as diamonds. (*He replaces it*)

Rupert enters with a baby

Rupert Hold this a minute and don't drop it.

Rupert pushes the baby, which is quiet, into Robin's arms and returns upstairs, where the other one is still crying

Robin stares at the baby

Rupert enters with the twin

They wanted a bit of attention. They would, of course, both women.

They pace the room, in opposite directions, passing each other en route

Robin In China, in the nineteenth century, when they gave birth to females, they used to drown them.

Rupert halts, appalled

Rupert Are you suggesting we should follow their example?
Robin (*halting*) Of course not.
Rupert We are not in China, nor is this the nineteenth century. (*He considers*) I wonder why they stopped . . .

They continue to walk

Don't jolt it.
Robin I'm not jolting it.
Rupert Given the slightest excuse they're invariably sick over your best suit.
Robin It isn't my best suit—it's my only suit. How long do we do this?
Rupert Half an hour.
Robin My arms ache already. My father advised me—never have children. Whether you're legally married or not, he said, they're always bastards.
Rupert As the mother of these innocent children is not legally married I consider that remark in dubious taste.
Robin Sorry.
Rupert Has it been sick yet?
Robin No. (*Pause*) Has yours?

Rupert sniffs

Has she . . .?
Rupert It's either that or your conger eel. Perhaps they need changing. Come on, let's investigate.

Rupert and Robin exit to the kitchen

Celia and Barry come in through the front door. Each has a brief-case. They seem very businesslike

Celia Rupert's probably gone shopping and forgotten to lock the door.
Barry Who has the airline tickets?
Celia I have.
Barry He won't be pleased.
Celia He will if we come back with our order books filled. Let's be sure we've got everything.
Barry You've got your passport, haven't you?

Robin enters. He has a bandage over his thumb

Robin Damn silly pins.
Celia Robin. Where's Rupert?

Robin indicates with his bandaged thumb

(*To Robin*) Barry Bingley-Brown. Barry, this is Robin Nightingale.
Barry That's my secretary's name.
Robin What is?
Barry Nightingale?
Robin You don't mean Helen?
Barry Yes, her name's Helen.
Celia It's not *your* Helen, is it?
Robin So it's you she's working for.
Barry She was with me a few years ago at Applebury's. Now I'm in partnership with Mrs Johns and—I ran across her a few days ago and she said . . .
Robin She wanted a career.
Barry Yes.
Robin Small world.
Barry Yes, it is. She's very efficient.
Robin So she tells me. I'm the new housewife. (*To Celia, indicating the kitchen*) He's the Guru. I'm the first disciple.
Celia I'd better pack. I'm flying to Paris.

Celia exits upstairs

Barry Don't you approve of your wife's working?
Robin I'm old-fashioned. I think a woman's place is in the home. Where's yours?
Barry At home.

Rupert comes in smiling

Rupert Damn silly pins. (*Seeing Barry*) Oh!
Barry How are you, sir?
Rupert Very well, thank you. Do you two know each other?
Robin Helen's boss.
Rupert No? Is he really? Where's Celia?
Robin Packing.

Rupert What do you mean, packing?
Robin I haven't the least idea. She said something about flying.
Rupert Flying?
Robin She mentioned Paris.
Barry Exports, sir.
Rupert How exciting!
Barry Yes, it is. Crochet-Rothschild got in touch with us. We've never exported to Paris before.
Rupert Are you saying Celia's flying to Paris? Leaving me with Karen and the kids?
Barry It's terribly important.
Rupert (*to Robin*) How do you like that, then?
Robin I see nothing wrong with it.
Rupert Oh, so you think it's all right?
Robin If she's running the business she's running the business.
Rupert You're very broadminded all of a sudden.
Robin Either she does it properly or she plays at it. Which do you want?
Rupert You make it sound very reasonable.
Robin I try to be fair.

Celia comes downstairs

Celia Darling, has Barry told you? Isn't it gorgeous?
Rupert I'm delirious about it. Mr Mug stays at home whilst you two trot off to Paris? I'm sorry if I appear less than ecstatic.
Celia Barry isn't going.
Rupert Oh, isn't he?
Celia Just me.
Rupert (*pleased*) Oh—well—the business must come first, of course.
Celia We're all driving to London Airport together, but Barry's going in the other direction.
Barry Edinburgh, sir. It's so much quicker by plane.
Celia I'm starving. Would you like a sandwich?
Rupert Smoked salmon—or caviare?

Barry indicates for her not to bother

Barry We shall fly back again on Monday.
Rupert We?
Barry My secretary and I. (*Pause*) Mr Nightingale's wife.
Robin Helen? Going with you to Edinburgh? It's the first I've heard of it.
Barry She's at home now, packing. No doubt she intended to tell you.
Robin Or, perhaps, leave a casual note on her dressing-table. Away for the week-end. Having a wonderful time. Love, Helen.
Barry I hope you don't object?
Robin Then I'm sorry to disappoint you. I do.
Rupert I don't see why. She's only doing her job.
Robin You've changed your tune.
Rupert One tries to be fair.

Robin Her place is with me, not gallivanting off to Edinburgh selling soap.
Rupert I don't know why you're making so much fuss about it.
Robin You didn't say that when you thought he was taking Celia.
Rupert No, but you did.
Barry Of course, if you object, she mustn't go.
Robin Then she'll say I've ruined her career. Life would be hell.
Celia (*to Rupert*) Darling, bring my case down.

Rupert goes upstairs

Barry I'm terribly sorry if you disapprove.
Robin It's all right. (*He is being sulky*) I shall manage, I suppose. It's just that I've made all sorts of plans. I'd rather Rupert doesn't know, but I've—(*hesitating*)—attended a couple of cookery classes.
Celia Robin, how clever of you.
Robin And tonight I'd planned—well—a rather special little dinner at home.
Celia But how sweet.
Robin Fish. Cooked in a way she's never seen before.
Barry Can you cook?
Robin (*being magnanimous*) 'Course I can. Oh, well, there'll be another time.

Rupert comes down with the luggage

Celia I think it's marvellous of you.
Rupert What's he done now? (*He puts down the luggage*)
Celia He was planning a marvellous little dinner party for Helen. Darling, it's time we were off. Come on, Barry, we'll miss the plane.
Barry I'm terribly sorry for lousing up your dinner party, sir. I'll give your love to Helen.
Robin Thank you very much.

Celia kisses Rupert. Barry takes the luggage. Celia goes out to the hall, then returns

Celia Darling, what's that awful looking thing staring at me over the side of a shopping basket?

Rupert glances at Robin. Celia realizes her error

Oh! Say good-bye to Karen for me. 'Bye, darling.
Rupert Good-bye.
Barry Good-bye.

Barry and Celia exit through the front door

Robin I'd better be going, too. To a broken home.
Rupert Helen doesn't know what she's missing. What a shame.
Robin What do you mean?

Rupert Something rather special for dinner.
Robin I don't know what you're talking about.
Rupert Cookery classes. (*He chuckles*)
Robin Oh! So we had our ear to the keyhole.
Rupert We happened to overhear.

Rupert reclines in the armchair and picks up a newspaper

"I'd rather Rupert doesn't know . . ."

Robin goes to the door

Oh, Robin—I shouldn't worry about Helen in Edinburgh. I'd trust Barry as far as I'd trust you. (*He roars with laughter*)
Robin I do trust her in Edinburgh.
Rupert Splendid.
Robin Mind you, I'd be less happy if I thought she was going to Paris. Alone with all those Froggies.

Rupert lowers his newspaper. Robin starts to go out, shaking his head sadly

Rupert Touché. (*He laughs*) Robin.
Robin Yes?
Rupert What are your plans for this evening?
Robin Reading a book. Watching the telly. Thinking. Being bloody miserable.
Rupert (*picking up a book*) Fresh asparagus. Fresh potatoes. Fresh garden peas. Fresh *Sole Colbert* fried in fresh breadcrumbs.

Robin is puzzled

Shall we say seven-thirty?
Robin Are you inviting me to dinner?
Rupert Why not? If we don't look after each other our immediate future is dim.
Robin It's very nice of you.
Rupert Do you like raspberry flan?
Robin Marvellous. (*Thoughtfully*) Fresh raspberries?
Rupert Naturally.
Robin I'll bring the wine. How about a couple of bottles of Chablis?
Rupert Make it three.

CURTAIN

SCENE 2

The same. A few weeks later, 7 p.m.

Rupert, Robin, Janet and Inga are discovered, all painting or drawing. Rupert's easel is downstage in the middle of the room, and it can be seen that he is responsible for a dreadful portrait. Karen is their model, seated, looking angelic, with a book on her knee. Drinks have been served

Robin Karen, darling, do keep still.
Karen I've been sitting still for hours. I'm as stiff as a stiff.
Inga I love the art class. It's given me a new lease of life.
Rupert I had no idea that painting was so easy.
Janet Head up, Karen. I've nearly got a likeness this time. (*To Inga*) It is fun, isn't it?
Karen It may be fun slapping paint on, but it's a bore sitting still. A good model has to be dumb from the neck up.
Robin You're a splendid model, darling.
Karen That's offensive. And it's seven o'clock. Time's up.
Robin Please sit still.
Inga It's only ten to.

The telephone rings. Rupert answers it

Rupert (*irritably*) R. H. Johns. . . . Yes, she's here. . . . There's no need to shout. You can't break off in the middle of a thing or you lose the magic. . . . I'll tell her. (*He replaces the receiver*)
Janet Mine or hers?
Rupert (*back at his easel*) I've no idea. (*He looks at Robin's picture*) You've given her a squint in the left eye.
Robin I haven't given her a squint in the left eye. If she has one she probably gets it from you.
Karen (*rising*) That settles it. Fifty pence each, please. Pay up.

They all pay her except Rupert

Robin Picasso would have given you three squints in three eyes.
Rupert It's amazing how you discover your vocation in life entirely by chance. I never guessed I'd so much talent.

Robin surveys Rupert's picture and laughs

And what's that supposed to convey?
Robin (*pointing at the picture*) What's that supposed to convey?
Rupert It's the best thing I've done yet. Her soul is laid bare on the canvas.
Robin Then I should cover it up.

They have paid Karen and are packing their equipment

Karen (*holding out her hand*) Daddy.
Rupert I sat in with the kids on Friday. Why should I pay you for sitting down when you don't pay me for sitting-in?
Karen (*looking at Rupert's picture*) No, I can't charge for that. (*She looks at Robin's picture*) Even if I do squint I don't squint in two opposite directions.
Robin That's how the artist sees you.
Inga (*to Karen*) Thanks, Karen, you did a good job.

Janet My God, it *is* seven o'clock. He'll be hopping mad.
Inga So what?
Janet So what?

They laugh

Celia enters through the front door

Celia (*calling*) Darling, I'm . . . (*She sees them all*) Oh.
Rupert Home? (*He looks at her thoughtfully*) Surely you're mistaken? I know the face, but . . .
Celia (*coming down into the room*) Don't be silly, dear. (*To the others*) Hello. I'd forgotten it was the Art Class. (*She looks at Rupert's picture*) That's awfully good. Who is it?
Rupert Whistler's Mother.
Karen Thank you.
Celia (*to Robin*) I called in at the office, but Helen went straight home from the station.
Robin (*puzzled*) Helen?
Celia She'll have been there a couple of hours now.
Robin Do I know someone of that name?
Rupert What was your wife called?
Robin Oh, her . . .

Janet and Inga say good-bye and rush out

Rupert Could it be she?
Robin Do you mean she's back again?
Rupert Just to keep in touch.
Robin I must see her while she's in town.
Celia I do hate sarcasm.
Rupert And how was Vienna?
Celia I haven't the least idea. I've been, as you very well know, to Birmingham.
Rupert I get so confused. I thought that was *last* week. And where are we next week?
Celia If necessary, darling, Bolivia. A miracle's happened. We're selling soap and making money.
Rupert Soap's going out and money's coming in.
Celia For the first time in years.
Rupert And at the same time our family life has gone down the drain.
Celia Oh, Rupert, it's only temporary.
Rupert It's rarely temporary when something goes down a drain. Once you've gurgled your way down that little plughole it's extremely difficult to gurgle your way up again.
Celia I work a twenty-four-hour day, darling. I do get tired of your grumbling.
Robin Did you say Helen was going to Bolivia next week?
Celia No-one's going anywhere next week.

Robin You're wrong. I am. I didn't get married for the privilege of being anchored to a kitchen sink.

Celia Neither did she.

Robin Then she should have said so at the time.

Celia Did you ask her? Robin, if a woman has ability, why should she waste it?

Karen Hear, hear. If men want cabbages they should marry cabbages.

Rupert I know who you've been listening to.

Karen Mummy. And she's right.

Robin A woman should make it clear what sort of vegetable she is before marriage, not after.

Celia How can she if she doesn't know? She's married before she has time to develop. She's unaware of her capabilities.

Rupert I'll admit there's something in that. I never knew I could paint.

Celia Let's stop arguing. You haven't kissed me.

Rupert kisses her

Rupert Welcome home.

Celia (*to Robin*) Robin, promise me when you see Helen you'll be nice to her. She's thoroughly worn out.

Robin Today, Celia, I came to a decision. I knew one day she might come back to me. One of our brief encounters, you know. She'd smile sweetly, and kiss me, and say "Oh, it's so nice to be home." And I knew I should do one of two things, one of which involved strangulation. Being a gentle creature, I chose the alternative. My car's outside and a toothbrush—and a pair of socks are in it. I've left home.

Celia You're joking.

Karen For ever?

Robin (*to Celia*) I'm not joking. (*To Karen*) For ever.

Celia But you can't.

Karen Of course you can't.

Robin (*to Celia*) Yes, I can. (*To Karen*) Yes, I can.

Celia Where will you go?

Robin I'll find somewhere.

Rupert You can stay here for a day or two if you're stuck.

Celia } (*speaking together*) { Where?
Karen } { Yes, where?

Rupert (*to Celia*) My study. (*To Karen*) My study. (*To Robin*) It's six feet one by six feet two. Used to be a broom cupboard.

Robin Sounds marvellous.

Celia Robin, I don't want to sound inhospitable, but I can't agree to that.

Rupert Oh?

Celia What would Helen think of me? I'd be conspiring to break up their marriage.

Rupert This is my house and if I say he can stay, you've no say in the matter.

Celia I certainly have. Because if you encourage Robin to leave Helen I shall leave you.

Rupert So that's it. (*Blustering but taken aback*) Fine. (*Pause*) Where will you go?

Celia I'll think of somewhere.

Rupert Oh.

Karen moves to the window

Robin I say, it's getting a bit out of hand, isn't it?

Celia It's no worse than your walking out on Helen. It's beastly of you to criticize her.

Robin She's an adding machine, not a wife. Anyway, she doesn't need me. The house is hers and all that therein is. If she's so happy with her soap she can hire someone else to run the house for her.

Celia She needs you.

Rupert When she comes home at night, tired, weighed down with problems and bank notes.

Robin You're breaking my heart.

Rupert I'll move my desk out of the study and fix the divan.

Celia Robin isn't staying here, Rupert.

Rupert But he is, if he wants to.

Celia Then I'm not.

Rupert Celia.

Celia exits upstairs

Karen (*looking through the window*) Rod—look who's there . . .!

Rupert Who are you swearing at?

Karen (*calling out*) Rod! (*Eagerly*) It's Rod. He's here. (*She hurries to the front door and opens it*)

Rodney enters. He is a large young man, thirtyish

Karen and Rodney embrace in the vestibule

How on earth did you get here?

Rod Train, sea, air, taxi.

They are kissing very happily

Rupert (*to Robin*) Who does she say it is?

Robin Rod.

Rupert That's what I thought she said.

Rupert takes off his jacket, rolls up his sleeves. Rod and Karen come forward, arms about each other

Karen Daddy, it's Rod. Rod, this is Daddy. And that's Robin. Oh, how wonderful. Why didn't you warn me? You should have phoned. You should have written. Oh, Rod.

Karen and Rod embrace again

Robin (*to Rupert*) Cool it, cool it. He'll murder you.

Rupert The bigger they are the harder they fall. (*He puts on his jacket*) However, violence—perhaps—is alien to my nature.
Rod How do you do, sir?
Rupert Hello.

Rod spreads out his arms

Rod Well, where are they? I want to see my daughters.
Karen They're asleep.
Rod Great—I'll catch them napping.
Karen Quiet, then. Just tip-toe in and out.
Rod Excuse us, sir.

Rod and Karen exit upstairs

Rupert If he wakes those two up I'll belt him one however big he is.
Robin He's a good-looking fellow.
Rupert Handsome is as handsome does. I shall reserve judgement until we've had a very serious discussion concerning his intentions.
Robin At least he's put in an appearance.
Rupert I'd an uncle who did that regularly. My aunt had six children and only saw him six times.

Rod and Karen come downstairs

Karen They're sleeping like little angels.
Rupert (*to Rod*) Good. Now, sir, perhaps you and I can have a few words together.
Rod Aren't they beautiful?
Rupert Who? Oh, delicious. Now, sir . . .

Celia comes downstairs with a suitcase

Karen Mummy, it's Rod. Rod, this is my mother.
Rod I can see that. (*To Celia*) I wondered why Karen was so beautiful. Now I know.

Rupert reacts

Celia She also gets her nice disposition from me and whatever common-sense she has. Do sit down. Has Rupert offered you a drink?
Rod No, not yet. (*He sits*)
Karen He likes Scotch and soda.
Rupert We haven't got any.
Celia I'll get it. (*She takes a bottle of whisky from the drinks cupboard*)
Rupert As I was saying—right now, sir, perhaps you and I can have a few words together.
Karen Rod, you look fabulous. So well. (*She pours Rod his drink*)
Rod So do you. You haven't changed a bit.

Rupert Well, allow me to tell you she's changed considerably since I last saw her in England. She's now a mother.

Karen and Rod are smiling at each other, as he takes his drink

Rod I beg your pardon. You were saying?
Robin Excuse me. I'll fetch my stamp album.

Robin goes out through the front door with a sigh of relief

Rupert I will repeat . . .
Karen I still think you should have phoned me.
Rod (*smiling*) I thought you liked surprises.
Rupert Well I don't, and . . .
Rod The very day my divorce went through I saw my boss and said "This is it. I'm on my way."
Karen Then you're free?
Rod Until you marry me.

Karen gives a cry of joy

Karen Oh, Mummy, isn't that marvellous? Daddy. (*To Rod*) Can we be married straight away?
Rod As soon as you say so. (*To Rupert*) That is, sir, if we have your blessing. It's customary to ask the young lady's father for her hand. I like to observe the formalities.
Karen Don't you worry about that, Rod, Daddy will give me away, won't you, Daddy?
Rupert A pair of carry-cots in the front pew should do that very nicely.
Celia Rupert!!
Rupert I am being asked to launch a ship that's already been torpedoed.
Celia You have got to give your consent. Daddy is very pleased. You've got to be pleased.
Rod (*raising his glass*) We'll do our best to make you proud of us. We'll be living in London. (*To Celia*) I hope that's all right, Mrs Johns? I don't want to do anything you disapprove of.
Celia (*startled*) Oh, yes.
Rod (*to Rupert*) And you, sir?
Rupert Oh, I'm glad it's got round to me. There are one or two questions I should like to ask.
Karen Belinda has put on two pounds.
Rod Is that good?
Karen And Sophie has put on one and a half.
Rupert (*loudly*) Excuse me, can you afford to keep a wife and two children?
Rod Good God, no. Who can these days? (*He kisses Karen*) We'll manage somehow.
Rupert My daughter is used to a certain standard of living. I don't wish to see it lowered.
Rod Don't forget, sir, at your age you're nearing the end. I'm just starting. Were you rolling in it when you got married?

Rupert I didn't have to be. We didn't start off with four mouths to feed.
Rod There you are, you see, you started in a small way.
Rupert Young people should wait until they're properly established before they rush into marriage.
Celia Are you telling them to wait?
Karen You were going to punch him on the nose if he didn't.
Celia Now you're telling him not to.
Rupert I think I'll have a drink. (*To Rod*) You're more used to this sort of thing than I am.
Rod This is the last time. I adore her. (*He embraces Karen. He turns contritely to Celia*) I hope I'm not shocking you, Mrs Johns?

Celia shakes her head and smiles weakly

Rupert It's refreshing to meet a member of the younger generation with such a tender regard for the proprieties.

A baby starts to cry upstairs. Karen goes to the stairs. Rod follows

Karen Ssh! She's probably crying in her sleep. Let's go and settle her down.

Karen and Rod exit upstairs

Rupert If ever I'm asked to recount the most embarrassing moment of my life, this is it.
Celia You're doing your best to stop the marriage.
Rupert I've always envisaged the day when someone would ask for her hand. I never imagined it would be interrupted by the bawling of their children upstairs.
Celia Face facts, Rupert. We want them to be married. At least he's willing. So many young people aren't these days.
Rupert He's in favour of marriage all right. He thinks you should do it every two years.
Celia Well don't try to talk him out of this one.

Karen and Rod come downstairs

Karen They're off again.
Celia Thank goodness for that.
Rod (*nodding*) Can we take it then, sir, that we're engaged?
Rupert (*through clenched teeth*) Engaged . . .

Rod produces a superb emerald ring

Rod Darling. At long last. Do you like it?
Karen Oh, Rod. Mummy. Daddy.
Celia It's wonderful.

Celia is staggered by its opulence. She glances at hers, then at Rupert critically, then puts her hand behind her back

Karen Oh, just look. (*She dances across the room*) Whoops! I'm engaged. Haven't we a bottle of champagne?
Rupert We'd no warning, if you recall, of this unique betrothal.
Karen Well you did the shopping this morning.
Rupert Unaware of the festivities to come the bottles I purchased contained cod liver oil and gripe-water.
Karen Oh, well, who cares?

Robin comes in with an overnight case, and leaves it in the vestibule

Robin, I'm engaged. (*She shows Robin the ring, and kisses him excitedly*)

Rod sits. Karen sits on the arm of his chair

Robin Congratulations. Good God, it's one of the Canadian Rockies.
Karen I want to be married in the village church.
Rupert Which village? Not ours?
Karen Well of course. You always said that's what you wanted.
Rupert Page boys, television cameras and two hundred guests, I suppose?
Celia Darling . . .
Rupert (*indicating the stairs*) We've already got a couple of bridesmaids, haven't we?
Celia Darling. (*She gives him a severe look. To Karen*) Perhaps a Register Office.
Karen You had a proper wedding.
Rupert Certainly we had a proper wedding—and you weren't there.
Rod I like to do things correctly. Still, it'd be quicker, I suppose. (*To Karen*) Why not?
Karen I always saw myself in a long white gown.
Rupert So did I. Unfortunately . . .
Celia Well, I'm glad that's settled.
Rod (*to Rupert*) Look, I want to assure you, Mr Johns, I mean to work hard at this marriage. As you know, my first was a flop. (*Pause*) Virginia and I started to quarrel right from the word go. (*Smiling at Karen*) She was the sort of woman who should never have got married. (*To Rupert and Robin*) She wanted a career.
Rupert (*to Robin*) One of those.
Rod Said I'd turned her into a cabbage.
Rupert I know the type.
Rod If there's anything I hate it's a career woman. I can spot one a mile off. Hard-faced. Masculine. Vinegary.
Rupert Do go on.

Rupert and Robin are pleased to let him go on. Karen rises and moves away from Rod towards Celia

Rod A woman's place is in the home.
Celia In the kitchen.
Rod That's right.
Celia Not wearing the pants.

Rod Virginia didn't see it like that.
Celia I guess she made your life a misery.
Rod She did. I told her "Man's the hunter. It's his job to go out and bring home the bacon."
Karen This, Rodney Billingham, is the latter half of the twentieth century. You don't hunt for bacon any more. It's all ready, wrapped up in supermarkets.
Rod I was speaking metaphorically.
Celia So you think a woman should stick to the trivia of domestic duties. Is that it, Mr Billingham?
Rod I wouldn't put it in those words.
Karen You'd just say "a skivvy" and leave it at that.
Rod Why, no.
Celia But that's exactly what you are saying.
Karen If you think I'm going to sit at home day and night you can think again.

Robin, with an embarrassed cough, exits through the outer door

Celia (*to Rod*) Is that what you expect?
Karen Always on tap? Awaiting my lord's return?
Celia Another cabbage?
Karen No thanks, Mr Billingham.

Rupert takes Rod's glass

Rupert May I refill it for you?

Rod nods gratefully

Scotch, wasn't it?

Rupert refills his glass. He taps the barometer as he passes it

Weather's taking a turn for the worse. I should tell you, Rodney, my wife is a very successful business woman.
Rod Oh, no. What *have* I said?
Rupert You have said, and I agree with you, that a woman should decide early in life whether she's a tycoon or a wife.
Celia Because, you see, Mr Billingham, unlike a man she can't expect to have her cake and eat it.
Rod (*to Karen*) Do you want a career?
Karen Well of course I do. What do you think I went to Canada for?
Rod You never mentioned it before.
Rupert That, if I may say so, is where you made the same mistake I did. You should have asked her.
Celia You should also have told her. Told her what you wanted was a maid, a nanny, a washerwoman, a lawn mower and a mistress rolled into one.
Karen If I get married I'm most certainly going to follow my career. Why do you think I got my typing speed up to twenty words a minute? (*She*

indicates the stairs) As soon as they're one year old I shall have a nanny.

Rod rises like a statesman about to orate

Rupert If I may make a suggestion. (*To Rod*) This is your big moment. Whatever you decide, stick to it. Your future depends on it.
Rod If she wants a career I think she should have one.
Celia How very understanding.
Rod But she can't have me as well.
Rupert Well said.
Celia Do you want them to get married or not?
Rupert Not if two years from today he's telling his third wife's father his first two were lousy career women who ruined his life.
Celia I'm not a lousy career woman. (*To Rod*) And I'm not vinegary.
Rupert True. But he's probably even better than you are. (*Indicating Karen*) And she's worse than I am. If they put her in charge of Marks and Spencers in two years they'd be back to a penny bazaar.
Rod I agree.

Robin comes in. He brings his overnight case into the room

Robin (*smiling*) How's every little thing?

They ignore him

Karen (*taking off her emerald ring*) Then you can take that back where you got it from.
Rod (*taking it*) If you say so.
Karen I do say so.
Rod All right.
Karen Right.

Karen and Rod turn their backs on each other

Celia (*to Rupert*) She's broken it off, and it's all your fault.
Rupert What have I done?
Celia You really are an idiot.
Rupert All I said was——
Celia You're a regular menace. A real home-wrecker. First Robin, now Karen. (*Indicating Robin's case*) Are you still going to let him stay here?
Rupert I can't go back on my word.
Celia Then as far as I can see there's no point in my staying any longer. I hope you're satisfied.
Robin Rupert, I can't allow you to quarrel over me.
Rupert Keep out of it. We'll decide who we're going to quarrel over.

Celia picks up her case

Celia Good-bye.
Rupert Good-bye.

Celia goes towards the front door

Karen Mummy, you don't think I'm staying here with them, do you? Oh, no. Come and help me to pack.

Karen and Celia go towards the stairs

Rod Do you mind putting me in the picture?
Rupert My wife's leaving me. (*Of Karen*) Your ex-fiancée's leaving you. (*Of Robin*) He's leaving his wife. (*Of Karen and Celia*) She's going with her. (*Of Robin*) He's coming with me.
Karen (*at the top of the stairs*) So now you know.

Celia and Karen go off upstairs

Rod Marvellous. I've sold my car, got a divorce, quit my job, vacated my apartment and travelled three thousand miles by land, sea and air. What about me?
Rupert Have you any plans?
Rod To get married, remember?
Rupert You'd better stay with us. You can share Karen's room.
Rod She won't be there.
Rupert With Robin.
Rod Thank you very much.
Robin I'm in the broom cupboard.

Rupert whispers in his ear

Sorry, study.
Rod Do you know something, Mr Johns? Your wife's right about you. You are a menace. You've just robbed me of the most beautiful thing in my life.
Rupert I've never robbed anybody out of anything. (*To Robin*) Have I?
Robin Only at cards.
Rod They're leaving us. Aren't you going to do anything about it? Well I am. I'm not going to stand by and watch it happen. I've come all this way to marry your daughter and I'm going to do it. (*He moves away*)
Rupert On her terms or yours?
Rod We'll negotiate. (*He starts to go upstairs*)
Robin You can't negotiate with women.
Rod If I can't handle them better than you two, I give up. (*Halfway upstairs*) My place is with my wife and children. You can always come to an understanding if you give and take.

Rod exits upstairs

Rupert If he gives and takes with Celia she'll have his shirt off his back. And how dare he blame us?
Robin You must admit he showed resolution.
Rupert I call it weakness, blaming other people. (*Pause*) I blame Celia.
Robin And Helen. They're both crackpots.
Rupert I'm all for equality, but on our terms. The ideal home has no bosses. Just the master and his mistress.

Robin I wonder how the negotiations are going?
Rupert Two to one against and one of them's Celia. They'll murder him.
Robin I get on quite well with Helen's mother. Mind you, she lives in Australia.

Karen appears on the stairs, excitedly

Karen Daddy, he's proposed to me again. I've accepted him. We're engaged again. (*She displays the ring on her finger*)
Rupert That didn't take long, did it?
Karen Rod's a man of action.
Rupert (*indicating the children, off*) We have proof of that, haven't we?

Karen exits upstairs

(*To Robin*) He's homeless, out of work and hasn't a cent. What a way to start.
Robin I saved up for years before I got married.
Rupert So did I.
Robin Seventy pounds in the bank.
Rupert I didn't do as well as that, but I had something in the Post Office.

Rod appears on the stairs

Rod (*excitedly*) We want to get married right away. With your permission, of course, sir.
Rupert There are still one or two questions I should like to ask.
Rod I'll make her real happy, Mr Johns.

Rod exits upstairs

Robin What were the questions, Rupert? Perhaps I can answer them.
Rupert I know the answers. Is he bust? Yes. Prospects? None. Can he foresee the glittering future you and I offered our wives? No.

Celia appears on the stairs

Celia (*sweetly*) Darling, you know that gorgeous little cottage in Lambs Lane. What's the name of the man who's selling it?
Rupert Robinson. And it isn't gorgeous, it's scheduled to fall down. And he isn't selling it because no-one in his right mind would buy it.
Celia I *am* relieved to know they'll be living so near. Do you realize, darling, you'll be able to see the children every day?

Celia exits upstairs

Rupert I'll see them every five minutes. You know what'll happen? She'll drag them round here and dump them on me. And when they're not here, I'll be there, propping up their tottering love nest. At first glance you'd say it was a derelict bus shelter. The main water supply comes through the roof.

Robin I suppose you noticed Celia's calling you "darling" again?

Rupert Isn't it marvellous? Sometimes it's impossible to enjoy a good row with Celia—she forgets you're having one.

Robin Nevertheless, I reckon you can take your morning suit out of mothballs.

Celia and the very loving couple come downstairs

Karen Oh, Daddy, I'm so happy.

Celia It's all settled, darling. You must see that man Robinson at once.

Karen I can't wait, Daddy.

Rupert Well I can. There is just one little point which some of us seem to have overlooked. Neither of them has a job, and I refuse to support them.

Karen But we have got jobs. You'll be thrilled when Mummy tells you. Tell him, Mummy.

Celia Darling, you've always wanted me to have a female secretary. (*Smiling*) I've got one.

Rupert Not her!

Karen Starting on Monday.

Rupert She doesn't know the difference between a filing cabinet and a nail file.

Celia She's promised faithfully to work hard. (*To Karen*) Haven't you, dear?

Karen Yes, I have.

Rupert Everybody's going to finish up working at Rupert Johns' Soap Factory except Rupert Johns. (*To Robin*) You see what they're up to? Whilst she's pecking away at a typewriter with two fingers Mr Mug becomes a full-time male Nanny.

Celia You're so wrong, Rupert.

Karen We don't want that at all, Daddy.

Rupert Then who is going to look after the kids?

Robin nudges Rupert and indicates Rod

Rod Well, as a matter of fact, sir—Mrs Johns thought—that is, Karen suggested—I mean, I decided . . .

Rupert You *did* negotiate, didn't you?

Celia So, until he gets a job, Rod's going to . . .

Rupert Stay at home and run the house?

Robin My God, it's catching.

Rupert shakes hands with Rod. Robin, on his other side, pats him on the back

Rupert Welcome to the Club. Congratulations—you got the better of them after all. Tell me—do you play cards?

Robin Can you paint?
Rupert How about cooking?
Robin I can let you have a marvellous fish recipe.

The Curtain starts to fall

Rupert You take half a dozen conger eels, swill them around in a couple of pints of beer . . .

the CURTAIN *has fallen*

FURNITURE AND PROPERTY LIST

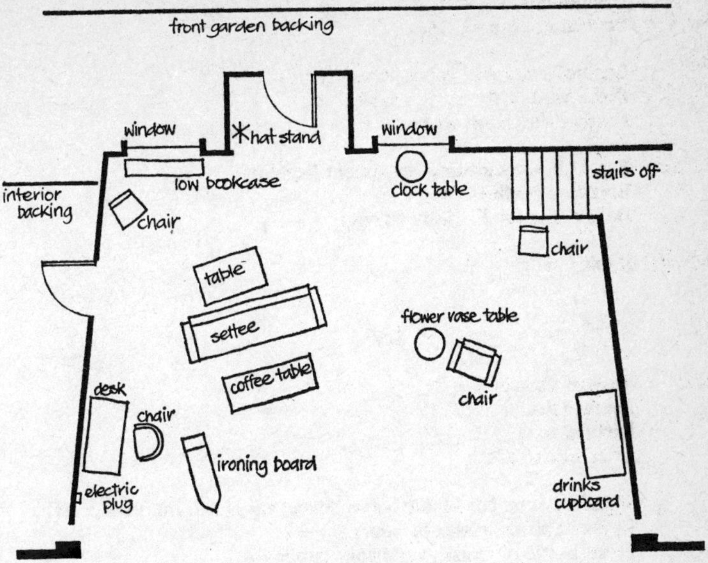

ACT I

Scene 1

On stage: Settee. *On it:* cushions
Armchair
Desk chair
2 small chairs
Settee table. *On it:* 2 vases (one to be broken), telephone, ashtray
Coffee-table. *On it:* ashtray
Occasional table. *On it:* vase of flowers
Small round table in window. *On it:* clock (to be broken)
Drinks cupboard. *On top and in it:* various glasses, decanter and bottle of home-made wine, bottle of whisky, soda syphon, other drinks
Desk. *On it:* writing materials. *In drawer:* diary
Bookcase. *In it:* books including several on cookery, silver medal in glass case
Ironing-board and iron with flex to wall plug. *On it:* clothes for ironing
On walls: painting, barometer
In vestibule: hatstand, hooks
Scattered around room: newspapers, magazines, clothing, laundry basket, cup, saucer, general untidiness
Carpet
Stair carpet
Window curtains

Off stage: Floorcloth **(Rupert)**

SCENE 2

Strike: All untidy articles and debris
Ironing-board and iron
Broken clock and vase

Set: Cushions straight, room generally tidy
Fresh vase of flowers on table
Feather duster on settee

Off stage: Bag of house-cleaning equipment **(Robin)**
Briefcase **(Celia)**
Bottle of special whisky **(Barry)**

Personal: **Robin:** badge

SCENE 3

Strike: Vase of flowers
Feather duster
Dirty glasses
Celia's briefcase

Set: 3 chairs round card-table below settee, cards and markers on table
Coffee-table in corner by stairs
Fresh bottle of whisky on drinks cupboard

Off stage: Briefcase **(Celia)**
2 carry-cots with "babies" **(Rupert)**
2 suitcases **(Karen)**

Personal: **Robin:** coins
Inga: coins
Janet: coins

ACT II

SCENE 1

Strike: Cards and card-table
Briefcase
Dirty glasses
Carry-cots
Suitcases

Set: Chairs in original positions
Coffee-table in original position
Ironing-board and iron as Act I, Scene 1
Children's toys and other appurtenances around room
Newspaper on armchair

Off stage: Shopping basket **(Karen)**
Peg basket and pegs, babies' nappies **(Robin)**
Shopping basket with eel, tins and packet foods **(Robin)**
2 "babies" in blankets **(Rupert)**
Briefcase **(Celia)**
Briefcase **(Barry)**
Bandage **(Robin)**
2 suitcases **(Rupert)**

SCENE 2

Strike: Ironing-board and iron
Children's toys and clothing
Pegs and peg basket
Shopping basket
Newspaper

Set: Easel down C with brushes, paints, etc. **(Rupert)**
Drawing-boards and materials **(Robin, Janet, Inga)**
Small chairs as required for painters
Book on settee for **Karen**
Drinks beside all on stage

Off stage: Overnight case **(Robin)**
Suitcase **(Celia)**

Personal: **Robin:** coins
Janet: coins
Inga: coins
Rod: emerald engagement ring

LIGHTING PLOT

Property fittings required: wall brackets, desk lamp (dressing only)
Interior. A living-room. The same scene throughout

ACT I, SCENE 1. Day
To open: General effect of late afternoon spring light
No cues

ACT I, SCENE 2. Day
To open: As Scene 1
No cues

ACT I, SCENE 3. Day
To open: General effect of early summer evening light
No cues

ACT II, SCENE 1. Day
To open: General effect of summer afternoon light
No cues

ACT II, SCENE 2. Day
To open: As Act I, Scene 3
No cues

EFFECTS PLOT

ACT I

SCENE 1

Cue 1 **Celia:** "Believe me." (Page 2)
Car approaches and stops

Cue 2 **Celia** exits (Page 5)
Crash of pots and pans

SCENE 2

Cue 3 **Rupert:** ". . . for Rupert Johns and Company." (Page 10)
Telephone rings

Cue 4 After **Rupert** exits to kitchen (Page 14)
Car approaches and stops

Cue 5 **Rupert** waves through window (Page 20)
Car drives away

Scene 3

Cue 6	**Rupert** receives money from card players *Telephone rings*	(Page 22)
Cue 7	**Rupert**: "You dealt, didn't you?" *Telephone rings*	(Page 22)
Cue 8	**Rupert**: ". . . finer qualities than others, that's all." *Car approaches and stops*	(Page 24)

ACT II

Scene 1

Cue 9	**Robin**: ". . . rice in a paddy field." *Sound of two babies crying*	(Page 35)
Cue 10	After **Rupert**'s exit *Reduce cry to one baby*	(Page 35)
Cue 11	After **Rupert's** second exit *Baby's cry stops*	(Page 36)

Scene 2

Cue 12	**Inga**: "It's only ten to." *Telephone rings*	(Page 41)
Cue 13	**Rupert**: ". . . regard for the proprieties." *Baby cries*	(Page 47)
Cue 14	**Rupert**: ". . . bawling of their children upstairs." *Baby's cry stops*	(Page 47)

MADE AND PRINTED IN GREAT BRITAIN BY
LATIMER TREND & COMPANY LTD PLYMOUTH
MADE IN ENGLAND